ADA – A VICTIM OF FATE AND CULTURAL CIRCUMSTANCES

ADA – A VICTIM OF FATE AND CULTURAL CIRCUMSTANCES

Barclays N Amadi

Book Guild Publishing
Sussex, England

First published in Great Britain in 2014 by
The Book Guild Ltd
The Werks
45 Church Road
Hove, BN3 2BE

Typesetting in Times by
Nat-Type, Cheshire

Printed in Great Britain by
CPI Group (UK) Ltd, Croydon, CR0 4YY

A catalogue record for this book is available from
The British Library.

ISBN 978 1 909984 69 1

Eternally dedicated to my God, the Almighty, for his mercies, and gifts of life, talents and love for me.

Everyone is a winner, but some of us are disguised as losers, so don't let their appearance fool you.

Contents

Acknowledgements

To my inspirational grandmother, Chief Esther Oyindah Amadi-Ichekwai, who always believed in me. I thank you massively for your undiluted love.

To my brilliant sweet mother, Chief Nwohuruakwu Iwai Amadi-Ichekwai – the supreme indomitable lioness with an indefatigable spirit, who defended us against an oppressive regime in a polygamous family. Thank you for your vision, enterprise and courageous efforts. I see my triumphant survival and accomplishments as the enduring legacy of your struggle and dogged efforts.

To my uncle and exemplary squadron leader, Chief Augustus Ihunda Amadi-Ichekwai, for choosing to make the sacrifices and commitments in order to fund my basic education at a time when resources were extremely limited. You led me to the mine path, showed me the gold mine and provided me with the necessary tools to mine the gold that is in my possession today. I am therefore eternally most grateful to you for providing the foundation pillars for my empowerment, personal development, ambitions and aspirations, which con-tinuously help me to access and explore a sea of opportunities. This book is just one testament in the list of many accomplishments that germinated from your priceless effort.

To all my children and wife – beauty extraordinaire, I

owe you all an enormous thank you for your unflinching support, understanding and love – individual and collective. I was physically absent at various stages when I was away gathering materials but at other times, when I was physically present, I was emotionally absent because I was engrossed in this project. I therefore plead guilty to being anti-social and absent both physically and emotionally. But as a reward, I invite you to regard this as the final product. I take my hat off to you all for showing me such degrees of tolerance and accommodation for acting out of character during this period.

To my most reliable confidant, Mr Innocent Ikechi Jonathan, a gentle giant whose advice, support and encouragement in my continuous quest for personal development were irreproachable. I hereby place on public record my full appreciation for being there for me.

To my brother Rev. C C Amadi, the spiritual leader whose guidance, prayers and support for the family have been relentless, I say thank you too.

To my darling sisters, Elizabeth Amadi and Mrs Carol Denson, what can I say to you? I am most grateful to you for making immense personal sacrifices and for your devotion in critical areas: for co-managing the special care, attention and love my mother needed during my absence as well as your commitments in my personal development. To my brother, Amb. Prince Musy Amadi and his lovely wife, Fortune, I salute you for your priceless support and for always being there for me.

To all other family members, I stand tall and rich to thank you for providing me with endless support and encouragement: Mrs Ndalu Amadi-Ngbeni, Comfort Amadi, Veronica Amadi, Dr Okechukwu S Amadi, Justice

Amadi Esq., Ndidi Amadi, Sheriff Amadi, Harry Amadi, Mr Sampson Denson and Mr and Mrs Wosu.

I also wish to extend my heartfelt thanks to my special family friends; Mr Ovunda Peter Amadi, Mrs Love O Glory-Joe, Mr Monday Wennah, Dr Tare Biu, Mr and Mrs Prince Vincent Atako, Mrs Egejuru Walker, Gold Opurum-Ukaegbu, T O Waamah Esq.,

To H.R.M Eze, ENB Opurum, J.P, MFR, The Ochie of Etcheland and his wife, Ogbeti Jeimimah, and Chief Ejike Marcus Chakara – Eze, Rumuchakara, for their endless support

Also, as every author would confirm, the long journey of any book from conception to publication requires team work. Many people with varied expertise work in a collaborative and cooperative partnership to develop a finished product. I therefore feel rich to thank the brilliant team at Book Guild and everyone that contributed to the realisation of my dream.

Lastly and most importantly, I am most grateful to all my readers – particularly all the millions of *Adas* out there – for inspiring me to write this book.

1

Brilliant Young Girl

Ada was a beautiful and happy young Nigerian girl who was popular with everyone around her due to her infectious smile and exemplary manner. She was known to be exceptionally brilliant, single-minded and self-motivated with an incredible independence of mind well beyond her years. She was also said to possess great determination, drive and energy – all key qualities for a future high-achiever. Surely, favoured by so many natural gifts, she was set to become someone successful and great.

She made her mark very early in school, where her talent and brilliance were soon recognised and appreciated. Unsurprisingly, she was head of her class for four years consecutively and the senior prefect in her final year at school. Ada was repeatedly nominated on merit to represent her school during inter-school debate and quiz competitions. Her prize-winning habit attracted huge media attention, which exposed her school to a wider audience. This in turn attracted overwhelming interest from parents within the school catchment area and beyond, to the extent that the school became a 'first choice option' for parents during the admission process. In appreciation of her contribution to the good name and reputation of the school, Ada was appointed school ambassador with a duty to advise prospective students and their parents during the admission process. News of her achievements at school spread through her home community and neighbourhood, where she became a popular celebrity, a role model and an inspirational figure to other young girls at a time when parents were reluctant to make investments in their daughters' education. Ada's astonishing accomplishments encouraged parents to educate their daughters, and within a short period of time her community witnessed an unprecedented increase in the number of young girls enrolled in schools.

Her parents, Mr and Mrs Okafor, hailed from a small village in the eastern part of Nigeria, but they migrated to a small but busy commercial town outside the main city in search of better opportunities. They were uneducated, petty traders and farmers with strong Christian beliefs, and were fondly known as 'good Samaritans' because they devoted much of their free time to community and church activities. This made them very popular and highly respected in the community. Despite their good reputation, though, they were known to be strict disciplinarians and hardcore traditionalists, who were very conservative in their understanding and application of traditional, cultural and customary values and practices.

Ada was the first of their five children and she was born after several childless years of marriage. After her birth, her parents experienced another difficult five years trying to have more children, to no avail. During this testing period, they became victims of their cultural and traditional belief that placed high value on male children over female children. Some sections of the community stigmatized, humiliated, ridiculed and abused them for the 'crime' of not producing a single male child. Others began to spread vicious rumours and made degrading and derogatory comments about them. Ada's mother, Ngozi, was rumoured to practise witchcraft and some said she had sacrificed all her unborn children in the process. There was a similar but equally untrue story that her father, Eze, was a member of a powerful secret cult and that he too may have sacrificed his male children. Some people accused the couple of offending the gods with their evil activities and argued that the gods had denied them male children as a punishment.

Their problem was further exacerbated by numerous close family members and friends who applied intense pressure on them to resolve their difficulties. Some advised the couple to seek the services of a *dibia* (native doctor) with a view to ask the gods what Ngozi might have done wrong, and in the process to ask for forgiveness and make any necessary sacrifice. Pressure was also applied by Eze's siblings, who advised him to marry another wife who would give him male children. He resisted the pressure, because such an action was not in accordance with his Christian faith. He considered the suggestion to be grossly offensive and unfair to his faithful wife. In any case, he was not convinced that this other wife would definitely give him male children.

More pressure came from Ngozi's family members, who advised her to seriously consider adopting a male child to avert the threat of her husband taking another wife. Again this idea was rejected without consideration by her husband, on the basis that it would provide more ammunition for rumour-mongers in their neighbourhood.

Furthermore, adoption carries with it a certain stigma in the community, because in Nigeria it has not yet attracted wider public acceptance. Eze also feared that men in the community would turn him into an object of caricature – accusing him of being incapable of fathering his own male children but only too happy to take another man's son. Similarly, women in the community might see adoption and failure to produce male children as concrete proof of Ngozi's incompleteness as a woman. Either way, the couple knew that it was a no-win situation for them.

Despite being subjected to such humiliation, abuse and pressure, the couple remained very philosophical in their understanding that they were victims in an unjust society. Although they understood the cultural and customary reasons why parents in their community yearned to have male children, they failed to understand why everyone would authomatically assume that it was always the fault of the woman if no male children were produced, or if a couple remained childless. Remarkably, Ngozi and Eze disregarded their challenges and remained faithful and grateful to God for blessing them with Ada, whom they cherished and regarded as a living monument of their love and the touchstone of their joy and happiness. Accordingly, Ada enjoyed lavish and unadulterated devotion, attention and care. They held the firm view that God would surely answer their prayer for more children when it pleased Him most.

That prayer was answered approximately five years after Ada was born, when the couple had their first male child, Chidi. He was followed by three more boys, with each new child coming approximately two years after the one before. The arrival of each of the boys ushered in

4

greater happiness and renewed hope for the family together with the corresponding financial challenges. The birth of their sons also brought the period of relentless humiliation and abuse to a natural end. With the pressure lifted from the couple's shoulders, they were able to concentrate on bringing up their young family. They regained their pride, respect and prestige in the neighbourhood and community. As the proud parents of four sons, they felt fulfilled at last: they had finally proved themselves to be worthy members of their society after all.

Even before the boys were born, Ada had started to exhibit signs of brilliance usually attributed to people categorized as 'genius'. Being bold and forward thinking in his outlook, her father felt the irresistible urge to provide Ada with the necessary tools to enable her to unlock her academic talents and, by extension, to discover and harvest her full potential in life. Consequently, they took a conscious and ground-breaking decision to make the necessary sacrifice and commitment to provide her with quality education up to university level. It was hoped at the time that a good education would guarantee her a better future, expose her to better opportunities and secure a good job for her at the end, which in return would help to transform the family's fortunes. Her parents made good their promise until Ada's sixteenth birthday, when the time came for her to leave the prestigious boarding school for girls she had been attending. They had funded her education through the family inheritance, with land and properties sold or used as collateral for borrowed money.

The decision to educate Ada was novel and risky, but it showed a remarkable courage on the part of her parents at a time when illiteracy was rampant, with many in the community choosing instead to imprison themselves in timidity and ignorance. Sadly, the society at the time held the view that any investment in the education and future of female children was a 'waste' of the family's valuable but limited resources. Ada's parents were subjected to ridicule, mockery and criticism for their decision to 'squander' family treasure and borrow large sums of money in order to educate Ada. It was to the detriment of their sons, they were told. Family members and friends questioned the wisdom of selling off a family inheritance meant for male children, only to spend it on Ada's education, after which she would marry and leave the family home for male children to manage. What was the point? But Ngozi and Eze simply set aside the advice and treated their critics with the disdain they deserved.

During her teenage years, Ada began to realize and appreciate the sacrifices and commitments her parents were investing in her education. Unfortunately, her parents' grand ambition to see her through university education was by then becoming increasingly unrealistic in the face of extreme financial difficulties. The family had always operated on a low budget to ensure survival for many years, and the size of the family had brought about a corresponding increase in both individual and collective needs. The unending pressure to balance the books as well as the need to satisfy competing needs had become more unbearable and stressful as the years passed. Inevitably, it created tension and had a negative effect on family relationships.

Faced with mounting debts on high-interest loans and with the loan repayments well behind, Ngozi and Eze were compelled to hit the brakes and take time to reconsider their position. They conducted a comprehensive review of the family's long- and short-term financial commitments, as well as their ongoing needs. At the end of this review, Ada's parents came to the inevitable conclusion that hard and painful choices had to be made.

It was no surprise to discover that spending on Ada and her education formed a substantial component of the family expenses. How were they to limit the family's financial exposure while at the same time balancing the long-term interests of both Ada and the family? One option was to ring-fence the cost of Ada's education and continue to fund it – but this would leave the family in financial tatters. The other option was to renege on the commitment to fund her further education. This option would shatter Ada's dreams and leave her feeling utterly devastated – but would help protect the family finances. Either way, the decision would be painful and the consequences unimaginable for the family and for Ada.

How should they decide? Ngozi and Eze turned to their knowledge of their environment, traditions, customs and culture for help. What were the different roles and expectations of men and women in Nigerian society? Reluctantly, on this basis, they came to the conclusion that Ada's education had become a necessary luxury the family could no longer afford. It was, they decided, reasonable to assume that Ada would marry one day and leave the family for good. It was not therefore reasonable to continue to fund her further education to the detriment of the entire family. The future of the family was paramount and must be secured. They were prepared to do their utmost to provide for and empower their four sons, who would be the future flag-bearers and chief custodians of the family name, inheritance and value, as well as fulfilling the male role of assisting the elders of the community to maintain the traditions, customs and culture.

Ngozi and Eze knew that the decision was difficult and painful, but they were convinced they had reached a considered decision that was best for both Ada and the family in the long run. Accordingly, they decided that Ada must marry as soon she left school, so that they could concentrate on providing and securing the future for their sons and the family name.

This decision prompted Ada's father to consider more seriously a proposal put to him previously by his creditor. This creditor had offered to marry Ada, and in return all the family debts would be written off and the land that had been used as collateral would be returned to the family. To Eze, this offer suddenly seemed very sensible, attractive and impossible to ignore, because it presented a once-in-a-lifetime opportunity for the family to liberate itself from all its financial burdens.

Meanwhile, it was the last mid-term break before her final year exams, so Ada was happily looking forward to returning home from school with some good news about her education. She was oblivious of the storm cloud gathering at home which would shatter her dreams and turn her world upside down.

One evening her parents summoned Ada for what she naively thought was an important meeting to discuss her progress at school. She was instead told that she would not be furthering her education as previously planned due to lack of finance and crippling family debts. Her parents provided her with an honest account of the family's financial problems, describing how the money was raised over the years to fund her education, the impact of this on the family finances and the future challenges facing the family. Ada was told plainly that the family had done everything it could for her, within its limits, and that attention would now be focused on preparing, educating and empowering her male siblings to manage the family long after she had married and gone away.

In addition to the family's financial difficulties, her parents also explained that their decision had been influenced by the traditional roles and expectations for male children in their culture. Men are the chief custodians of our tradition, culture and custom, Ada was told. They inherit, manage, maintain and protect all the family possessions – landed properties (including farmland) and other valuable possessions – with a duty to hand down all inherited family possessions to the next generation. They manage the general affairs of the family, with the eldest son acting as head after the father's death. They maintain the name of the family and the lineage by producing male children of their own. They form into groups of a similar age (known as age groups), and at the appropriate age they contribute (financially and otherwise) to the proper administration of the immediate and nuclear family, and at compound and village level, to the maintainance of peace, security, unity and development. They are responsible for claiming all entitlements due to the family – for example, free farmland and land to build residential homes. Traditionally they also look after their parents in old age.

By contrast, Ada was also told what society and tradition expected of women. They marry out of their family homes as soon as they are considered old enough to do so, depending on cultural variations. Once married, they are usually not expected to return to the family except on occasional visits or to attend weddings, burials and other special events. Divorce is usually considered a taboo because it brings shame to the woman's family, and she would risk losing everything, including her home and children, and her family would be expected to return the bride price. Divorcees are stigmatized and find it extremely difficult to get another husband. Women are expected to channel all their activities, resources and energy into building and developing the marital home, and all rights and privileges reserved for married women must be accorded without exception. Wives must, however, accept automatic forfeiture of rights and privileges (such as inheritance) and are generally exempted from certain responsibilities and obligations designed to aid development of their father's home or community. However, any assistance is usually voluntary, subject to permission from her husband. Failure to seek such permission, or if the permission is refused but the wife proceeds to carry out the project regardless, may invite a serious domestic situation leading to dire consequences.

Horrified by what she heard, and sensing finality in her parents' position on the matter, Ada went down on her knees and pleaded with her father not to give her away in marriage at such a young age. She tried to persuade them to consider the benefits to the family if she completed her education and secured good employment. Her father told her, however, that this was no longer a viable option and had already been considered and discarded. Marriage was the only option available. She should know, her father said, that the family had arranged for a wealthy and prominent man (who happened to be the family creditor) to marry her.

In return, the man had promised to let her further her education, to write off all their debts, to return the family land and to assist her brothers.

Ada hastily requested another urgent meeting with her mother, hoping for a different reaction in private, hoping to win her understanding and support as a woman. Her mother told her that in an ideal world she would have preferred Ada to complete her further education before considering marriage. Sadly, the family did not live in such a rosy and perfect world where all expectations were fulfilled. She instead emphasized, with a touch of softness, that the family operated in a world ravaged by endless poverty, unfairness, uncertainty and inequality. She invited Ada to understand the underlying family predicament and to accept the decision as the best one for her and the family in the circumstances. Her mother added that if funding her further education was possible, then they had demonstrated by their commitments and sacrifices thus far that they would have gladly accepted the challenge without any iota of hesitation. She urged Ada to consider herself and her generation very lucky to have experienced some level of education, because she herself had married at the age of sixteen without any form of education at all. In her day, she told her daughter, nearly every family was impoverished: education was an expensive commodity that made it the preserve of wealthy families, or of male children in working-class families with limited income.

Ada looked her mother straight in the eye and asked, 'So it's all about male children?' Ngozi nodded reluctantly. Ada was offended: she was intellectually superior to some boys of her age and therefore failed to see why men should be treated as special.

She asked again, 'If I was the first son, and given the same financial difficulties, would your decision have been different?'

Her mother pleaded with her to understand that it was not all about intellectual ability alone, but cultural roles and expectations of men in a traditional family set-up had to be factored in as well. If Ada had been a boy, her mother said they would have considered two options. The first option would have been to terminate the first son's educational ambitions at the same level as Ada's, but he would have been required to secure a job and suspend starting his own family for a few years in order to assist his parents in running the family affairs. This would have included the responsibility to fund his brothers' education, as expected by tradition.

This was simply not a viable option for Ada, she said, because they did not have the choice and luxury of time to delay her marriage or to bar her from starting a family for several years due to biological and cultural reasons. For example, pressures would naturally come from men asking for her hand in marriage, and if she persistently declined the marriage proposals – even if for perfectly good reasons – over time people would naturally become suspicious about her and she would run the risk of ending up without a husband at all. Such an unpalatable position would subject her family to humiliation and shame. Additionally, Ada would ordinarily be expected to marry once she was of the right age, unless there were legitimate reasons against it, such as being in full-time education. So, if Ada was not in full-time education, it would be very difficult and embarrassing for her parents to justify why she was still at home. Concerned family members and friends would ask disturbing, probing questions, while rumour-mongers would do their utmost to make life very uncomfortable for the family by spreading vicious stories about Ada, her parents and her family.

The second option would have been to assist the son to acquire university education, but that would have meant stretching the family resources to the very limits and inevitably exposing the family to greater expense and suffering. Her mother further added that adopting this second option might have resulted in one or two of his siblings receiving little or no formal education as a sacrifice for the greater good of the family. The good news about this option would be that the first son would automatically become the 'family breadwinner' and he would be expected to make greater sacrifice for the family in accordance with tradition and custom. He would be expected to secure a job and work for many years to help clear the family debts, fund the costs of his brothers' education and fulfil other family obligations before he settled down to marry and have his own children. Again, Ada was told that this option would have been highly prejudicial to her interests and certainly not attractive to the family due to some critical determinants like financial, moral, social and cultural barriers – namely, her age, biological clock, the roles and expectations of women in her society, and loyalty to her marriage.

Her mother then went out of her way to provide a graphic explanation of all the financial intricacies that would have been involved in funding her university education, as well as the cultural complexities after her graduation. By the time she finished both her university programme and the national youth service, Ada would be in her mid-twenties. In the ordinary course of events, both the family and the wider society regarded this age as the prime time to marry, with pressure and expectation for women graduates to marry usually at fever pitch. Failure or delay in marrying at that age was viewed with a high degree of suspicion. If a woman was not yet married between the ages of twenty-eight and thirty, it set off alarm bells in the minds of her parents, triggering probing questions and further pressure. Her mother gave Ada two scenarios to help her understand better the level of risk the family might be exposed to if they proceeded to help her achieve her desire for a university education.

Scenario number one involved a situation wherebyAda got married soon after graduating from university to a young man of her choice who shared a similar poor background. Culture and society expected that primary loyalty to her marriage and responsibility to her married home ought to take precedent over loyalty and duty to her father's home. This would mean that Ada forfeited the automatic freedom to render favours to her family whenever it pleased her. Ada would need to obtain permission from her husband before acting in that way. If she asked for permission and it was refused, or she failed to ask for permission before offering to help her family, she might run the risk of creating an explosive domestic situation that she would find difficult to handle. Such a situation would inevitably leave both Ada and her parents very vulnerable. She would be unable to assist her parents to repay the money borrowed to fund her education, or to make any contribution towards her siblings' education, thereby exposing her family to financial ruin. However, if her parents took such risks with a male child, they would not face such a terrifying prospect.

The second scenario related to a position where Ada decided to postpone marriage for years in order to work and retain her freedom to help her parents and siblings. Her mother informed her that this option was unattractive because at the end of that period she would be into her thirties. Her biological clock might kick-in, thereby occasioning fertility problems, which in turn might pose further difficult challenges for her in the marriage. The extended delay might also cause her to find it more difficult to attract a husband. If the latter were to be the case, Ada's parents were concerned that this scenario might cause them to have an unmarried, grown-up woman at home, with the horrible prospect of Ada having children out of wedlock. Her mother ended by saying again that they had carefully considered all the options and the implications before reaching the very difficult and heartbreaking decision not to fund her further education.

Ada was naturally very devastated and disappointed after the meeting. She was left feeling very lonely, vulnerable and betrayed by those who claimed to love and protect her. She spent days in self-imposed solitary confinement in her room, crying and refusing to eat. She questioned herself over and over again. 'Why was I born a girl in a man's world? Why am I a victim of culture and tradition that places such a high premium on male over female children?' Ada could not understand the logic behind such discriminatory attitude towards women, particularly as she had proved to be academically superior to most boys of her age.

She imagined the effect on herself of not accomplishing

her academic ambition and potential in life. She contemplated her fear of having children in her teens, of getting married to an older man, possibility of suffering domestic violence and rape in marriage, and all the other burdens associated with marriage as a teenager. She imagined how all these could be happening to her at a time when her friends and classmates would be studying and preparing themselves for a better future. She considered suicide, but discarded the idea because it seemed so defeatist. She decided instead to live, and to fight for her freedom.

Ada went back to school after the short break feeling very angry that her life was taking such a turn for the worse. At school she adopted an attitude that was considered by her friends and everyone who knew her to be wholly inconsistent with her normal behaviour. Ada was no longer that bubbly, happy, easy-going girl with the infectious smile and energy. Instead, she became very reclusive and ostracized herself from her close friends. Crucially, her academic work began to suffer as she started recording marks below her usual high grades, and this did not escape the notice of her teachers. However, every effort made by her teachers and friends to identify the underlying cause of her problem was treated dismissively or was simply waved away with a smile.

Being the most brilliant student they had, Ada was naturally expected by the school establishment to make them proud by achieving the best O Level results in comparison to other schools in the area. It was hoped that this would enhance the reputation of the school as a centre of excellence, thereby attracting quality students in the future. But the school was understandably fearful that her recent behaviour might cause damage to the school's reputation, and that compelled the matron to draw the matter to the attention of the school head. Ada duly went to see the head, and with her usual smile and charm managed to mesmerize him into accepting a concocted story designed to mask her personal difficulties without revealing anything of note. Ada promised to change for the better and to make the school proud with good grades. She completed her final exams on the last day of the term and said farewell to her friends with a heavy heart, knowing full well that her educational ambitions had come to a dead end.

2

The Fight for Freedom

Ada returned home from school after her final O Level exams in combatant mood, ready to begin the long road to self-liberation from the clutches of poverty and tradition, which seemed to her designed to oppress women and hold them in bondage. Ada was convinced that lack of money had always been a weapon of choice in the armoury of her society – a weapon which could be easily deployed at any time by any interested parties within that society, to the detriment of women and their development. It was particularly so wherever there was clear evidence of competition in the family, when hard choices had to be made between the needs of male and female children. In such cases, Ada concluded, poverty was automatically given disproportionate weight by the family adjudicator, who would use the lack of resources as a convenient shield to satisfy the needs of male children over female children. Ada genuinely believed that her parents were hiding behind poverty in their determination to sacrifice her developmental and educational needs in order to secure a better future for her brothers.

Her view was simple: the plot was for her parents to ship her away from the family home in the interests of marriage at a tender age. Ada resolved to rebel and challenge her parents' decision to force her into an arranged marriage. She was determined to use every traditional and customary method of dispute resolution available to her, but her knowledge of those traditions and customs was understandably deficient due to her age. To navigate her way through this difficulty, she quickly commissioned her mother to help her. Accordingly, her mother explained to her all the customary routes and levels of complaint, their respective powers and sanctions, and the different methods of lodging complaints and appeals.

It turned out that there were five levels of appeal which she might have to work through one by one. They ran as follows: open and frank discussion with her father; complaint to her father's siblings; complaint to wider family elders (in a nuclear family set-up); complaint to the compound elders (chiefs); and finally complaint to the wider village elders (chiefs).

Following this illuminating discussion with her mother, Ada convened a meeting with her father. She wanted to see if he had changed his mind, and if not, to offer him one last opportunity to do so. To her disappointment and horror, her father stood his ground and used the opportunity to reveal that a meeting had already been arranged with her proposed husband to discuss traditional wedding arrangements.

Ada asked her father, 'Did you ever love me? And if so, why are you willing to stop my education, and why are you determined to give me out in marriage at a tender age to an older man?'

Burying his head in his hands, her father replied, 'Yes, I have always loved you very much. I have made painful sacrifices to prove that in the past.' But just as he had previously done, her father sought refuge in poverty and went on to regurgitate traditional and customary values to justify his actions.

By now Ada was convinced that her father was very serious. There was no going back as far as he was concerned. Aggrieved by her father's entrenched position and fearing that she had entirely failed to persuade him to change his mind, Ada declared all-out war. She knew that her options were either to accept her father's decision or to defy it. She took some time to consider carefully the risk exposure points, the benefits and the associated consequences of each option.

The first option was to do nothing, but to accept the dictates of a culture that saw women as commodities, undermined women's personal development, encouraged the limitation of choices available to women, suffocated women's ambition, oppressed and degraded women, abused women's rights and privileges, treated women as second-class citizens and held them in perpetual bondage. Ada instantly discarded this option without further consideration. In her view, it meant doom, gross injustice, helplessness and hopelessness, turning generations of women into the living dead from the moment of their birth.

She preferred the second option, which was to take up the fight for justice, liberation, freedom and equality for women, in the hope that other women would be encouraged to join her in the battle. But challenging or disobeying her father meant taking on the establishment – and most in her community would consider that unthinkable. The repercussions for herself, her parents and her family were unimaginable. She was aware that she would be demonized as a rebel and non-conformist by a community that placed a high regard on respect and considered marriage as an important institution. Accordingly, it was a given that every woman ought to be proud of marriage and must aspire to be married in order to bring pride, joy and happiness to herself, her family and community. Refusing to marry was therefore shameful, disgraceful and abominable conduct liable to cause terminal damage to her parents, her family and all the women in her community.

Ada was also only too aware that demonization was just a tiny part of the price she would pay for her actions. Her reputation could scare men away from coming to ask for her hand in marriage, which in turn might cause her to lose some rights and privileges in the community if she chose to remain unmarried. She could be excluded from all clubs and activities which were exclusively reserved for married women. If she decided to have children outside marriage, those children would be regarded as bastards and, in the case of male children and their offspring, they might suffer identity crises and lose some rights usually accorded to male children in her father's family. Ada would almost certainly have to impose self-exile upon herself by moving to a city outside her home community.

Furthermore, Ada knew that the stigma would result in unending embarrassment, humiliation, gossip and innuendo for her family. Her father enjoyed immense popularity and respect in the community, but Ada's rebellious behaviour would affect his credibility and undermine his influence. The community would see her parents as weak and unable to guide, train and discipline their wayward daughter. Ada's refusal to marry the man her father arranged for her would also mean he would still have huge debts hanging over his head and might possibly lose his farmland and other family inheritance he had used as collateral to borrow money to fund her education.

For generations of Ada's wider family, perhaps more humiliation and damage would descend when men came to her father's immediate and extended family to marry. Ada knew that it was customary in her community for prospective fathers- and mothers-in-law to conduct 'due diligence' on the bride's character, family background, discipline and demeanour – with a view to revealing any propensity to commit adultery, or any history of divorce, reprehensible behaviour or other misconducts. This information was usually provided by neighbours or family friends before any marriage. Her disobedience and insubordination, coupled with her decision not to marry, would therefore cause long-lasting damage to anyone connected to Ada – her siblings, cousins and nieces for generations to come.

Ada also reminded herself that tradition granted her father the supreme right to give his consent to and accept her marriage dowry (bride price) when she wanted to marry. Without this, the marriage could not happen, and if it went ahead without his blessing, it would not be recognized. As a punishment for the humiliation and pain she would cause him by refusing to marry the man he had arranged for her, her father might ultimately use this deadly weapon against Ada when she wanted to marry the man of her choice. This meant that Ada might never be married in the traditional way, which was one of the most important, celebrated and indispensable parts of her culture. Traditional marriage was fully recognized, respected and highly valued in her society and it was seen as the ultimate pride of a woman. It was one of the few special days when family members, friends and the wider community gathered to witness the father giving his daughter away to the groom in the presence of the groom's family and members of the public. If her father refused to give his consent for Ada to marry the man of her choice, there would be no dowry and she would miss the traditional wedding spectacle, as well as the associated rituals, happiness, joy and pageantry of that colourful, once-in-a-lifetime occasion.

Of course, Ada had the option to leave her family and migrate to a different city to live and work and, if opportunity presented itself, she could have a secret marriage in court or church without the consent, authority and attendance of her parents, family members and friends. Yet while such a marriage would be perfectly legal, Ada knew that marriage without the authority and support of her family would leave her vulnerable and isolated, thereby exposing her to exploitation and abuse in the relationship. Ada also knew that the court or church wedding would not erase the fact that her dowry had not been paid and therefore she would have to carry that baggage for the rest of her life. Such a deficit might be converted into a potent weapon by her husband, or by her enemies in the wider society, in order to abuse, humiliate, taunt and mock her in the future. She would potentially be setting up a time bomb.

After reviewing her options and the associated consequences, Ada concluded that she must take control of her life. She would not let her father shape her destiny. She felt that her freedom and rights were more important to her than anything else. She understood the extent of the pain, hardship or isolation she might suffer as collateral, but she was determined to endure any fallout that occurred as a consequence of her decision. She also felt that enduring the consequences of her freewill actions was far better than suffering life in a forced marriage. Ada was also fully aware that she would be alone, that the risk was very high and that the task was Herculean and nearly impossible. She also reminded herself that she might be hurt, frustrated, humiliated and treated with a high degree of ignominy. She was fully aware that the terrain would be rough, tough, full of obstacles and most difficult to navigate. But she was determined and motivated to fight, knowing that this was a generational struggle for freedom without any time limit. If she failed or was defeated along the way, then another woman or group of women would be encouraged by her efforts to carry the fight forward to the next level.

After the unproductive meeting with her father, and fully aware of the scale and dangers of her chosen option, Ada decided to escalate the fight to the next level in accordance with the customs her mother had described to her. She therefore summoned her father before his immediate family members – one older brother, two younger brothers and a sister. At the meeting, Ada was called on to state her case. Representing herself and drawing on the presentational, debating and advocacy skills learned at school, Ada eloquently and confidently presented her case with a mixture of passion and emotion that astonished her audience. She emphasized the two offending points: the decision not to allow her to go on to further education, and the plan to force her into an arranged marriage at the age of sixteen to an older man she did not know. She conceded that the family were poor, and that the family had built up its debts to fund her basic education, which no doubt had influenced her father's decision to halt her further education. However, she protested strongly against the idea of a forced or arranged marriage, which she considered to be highly offensive and unreasonable in view of her age. She made an emotional plea to her parents and the community to grant her full protection and sufficient time to reach maturity and gain the necessary experience needed to cope with the tribulations and responsibilities associated with married life. She closed her case by inviting her parents to allow her the option of securing a job in order to save up for her further education.

Ada's father reiterated his love for his daughter and maintained that he would do whatever it took, within his limits, to help her achieve the very best for herself. He added that he had shown such a level of commitment in the past by his words and deeds. He said the decisions he had made were difficult and painful, taken with a heavy heart after careful consideration of the options available in the best interests of his family. He confirmed that Ada knew the factual basis for his decisions as well as the logic behind them, and that the decision to stop her education was due to lack of money and nothing more. As for the marriage, he told his siblings that Ada had finished her education and should therefore look forward to marrying the man the family had arranged for her, because she was now of age and could not afford to stay idle at home.

After hearing from both parties, the family unanimously ruled in favour of Ada's parents. They expressed satisfaction that her parents had offered Ada a level of education rarely seen for girls in their community. They were therefore very grateful to Ada for utilizing the opportunity to bring pride and joy to the family and community through her academic brilliance. However, they concluded that the sacrifices and commitments made by her parents came at a price, because they had breached their financial limits and borrowed money, giving rise to heavy debt to such an extent that the family now faced financial ruin. This was a clear demonstration of commitment which Ada ought simply to be grateful for, because few parents in the community would be willing to make such a level of sacrifice for their daughters. The family ruled that Ada's parents could not support her call for further education, on the basis of lack of funds to prosecute such a gigantic project. As to marriage, the family unsurprisingly held that Ada was now of age and mature enough to marry the man who had been carefully chosen for her by her parents. The family cited numerous examples of girls from many generations before Ada who had married at her age with no formal education whatsoever. The aunt confirmed that this age-old practice was not new and that both herself and Ada's mother were living examples.

Ada took her time over the next two days to reflect on the judgement and the reasons given. Apart from the fact that the decision went against her, Ada was alarmed to learn that her situation was so prevalent in the community. It had become a standard practice for women to marry early without any formal education. After careful consideration, Ada came to the conclusion that her family had misdirected itself in reaching a decision she felt was so perverse, unreasonable and manifestly wrong. Surely a reasonable jury properly directed would not have reached the same conclusion? The family's decision, she thought, was tainted with bias in favour of her father simply because he was 'one of them' and they lacked the courage to disagree with him. Crucially, Ada was concerned that their decision was contaminated by their knowledge and experience of past events – a shared background which had become sufficiently powerful and influential to control their thinking, to the extent that it impaired their ability to think 'outside the box'. She concluded that their judgement was clouded by their belief in traditional, cultural and customary practices. They had become enslaved by these practices and were not able to extricate themselves from their cultural prison in order to accommodate change. Finally, the family had apparently failed to consider all the material points when reaching their decision. For example, as an alternative to marriage at a young age, Ada had proposed that her parents allow her time to gain employment and earn money in order to help save up for her education as well as gain more experience and maturity. They had disregarded that suggestion. Equally, the idea that arranged or early marriage was a serious moral and human rights issue was also conveniently ignored in their deliberations. For these reasons Ada strongly believed that the family had made a wrong decision, and that gave her sufficient grounds to take the matter to the next level of appeal.

Still feeling incandescent with rage at not getting justice from the immediate family hearing, Ada appealed to the wider family elders, in the hope that these more liberal-minded figures would be more understanding, sympathetic and flexible in their approach to their traditional and customary practices. She therefore summoned her father before the larger nuclear Okafor family, headed by the grandfathers. The hearing date was conveniently placed on a Saturday evening to allow everyone to attend. Her father received a formal notification of the summons and immediately flew into a rage. He had considered the matter closed after his siblings reached what he thought was a final determination of the matter. He couldn't understand why Ada had embarked on a course of action apparently designed to damage his credibility and undermine his standing in the community.

The meeting was fully attended by grandfathers, fathers, uncles, cousins and nephews from different generations. Ada felt frightened and intimidated when she arrived to see a sea of people gathered and waiting for her. The customary protocol was very impressive to her, and in some ways a joy to observe. However, she quickly gathered her thoughts and drew on her public speaking experience from her school days. Ada and her father were both called on to present their respective cases. Both basically repeated the submissions they had made at the last hearing. After due consideration, the elders again found in favour of Ada's father, on the same grounds as before.

Ada sought and was granted permission to make a second submission to the elders. She reminded the larger nuclear family and the community that both bodies had scholarship funds in place for the benefit of children in the community, with awards usually being made on merit to the most brilliant scholars. Ada invited the family and the community to consider her for an award, since it was on public record that she was the most brilliant student of her generation in the community, and her achievements had undoubtedly enhanced the name and reputation of that community. The family responded by expressing its gratitude to Ada for her contribution to the family and community at large. However, her request was refused on the basis that the scholarship fund was reserved for males only, because they would remain in the family and community to help develop it after their time in education, while the females would naturally marry and depart to their husbands' homes.

Ada challenged the elders to be more tolerant and flexible in their approach in order to accommodate a rapidly changing world. She added that some of the traditional and cultural beliefs in Nigerian society were terminally flawed, both in conception and execution, and as a result had brought about demonstrable errors in the decision-making process and lamentable systematic failures in the wider society. The sun had already set, she told them, on some of the more archaic beliefs, especially the idea that equipping and empowering female children of the family through education before marriage would only bring benefits to their husbands. She further argued that traditional beliefs and expectations which seemed to quarantine and restrict women's role in society to mere housewives had been obliterated by modern life in the world at large, including Nigeria, which was driven by improved technology, raised living standards and increased choices, rights, roles, duties, responsibilities and expectations of women. This meant, she explained, that women were now more mobile and flexible, with realistic expectations of making immense contributions in the development of society in areas such as commerce, environment, economy, politics and sports, in addition to their traditional household functions.

Ada was obviously very disappointed and frustrated after the hearing, burdened with a mixture of rejection and dejection. She could not understand why her family and community – who supposedly owed her a duty of care to protect her interests and guarantee her rights – had so woefully failed to move with the changing world. Instead they had opted to hold steadfastly to old-fashioned views they thought to be immutable. Some of the views of her people were manifestly inconsistent with a modern outlook, and the elders had failed at a time when openness and clarity of thought were needed most.

Ada returned home to reflect on the implications of the judgement and to consider her next line of action, which in theory involved taking her case up to compound and village levels. However, she questioned the wisdom of going to those levels if the elders were from the older generations and were therefore bounded and imprisoned by the same old beliefs and practices in culture, custom and tradition. With no options left for her within or outside her community, Ada was left feeling very isolated and vulnerable. Although she had always known that the task ahead was not going to be easy, at this stage she found herself surprised by the enormity of it and particularly by the depth of resistance to change.

While Ada was busy reflecting on an already difficult situation, additional complexity was introduced which had a profound and negative effect on her struggle. She was told that rumours were fast spreading in the community which alleged, amongst other things, that she was tarnishing the name and image of her father and the family by her conduct. Soon, Ada was facing unprecedented pressure from all directions – starting with her mother, aunt and close family friends – to accept the situation and look forward to a happy married life.

Some days later, her father hauled her in and demanded to know why she was determined to drag his name through the mud so unnecessarily. He repeated how he had sacrificed all in the face of abject poverty to provide her with the best education, even going beyond his means to do so. He added that at the time, some family members and friends had discouraged him, warning him that he was acting outside the traditional norm and that his actions would one day come back to haunt him. Her father further recalled that people at the time had accused him of wasting money on educating a girl who would merely marry into another family, instead of saving the money to provide education for his male children.

Crucially, he reminded Ada that people had confronted him at the time and demanded to know why he was equipping her with knowledge and the dangerous weapon of education that she might later use to challenge her husband or the traditional values. But he had resisted the pressure and the advice because Ada was so academically gifted, and he had been encouraged by the church pastor at the time to help her develop her potential for a better future. Sadly, her father now said that he was beginning to think the prophetic words of his friends were becoming a reality, judging by Ada's recent conduct. He warned Ada to stop her unruly conduct and to control her obsession for further education, and instead to concentrate on getting married. She was told in no uncertain terms that if she continued with her appeals, or maintained her refusal to marry the man the family had arranged for her, she would be expelled from the family home and disowned, and consent would not be given for her to marry a man of her choice in the future.

With her back to the wall and faced with the threat of losing her family, Ada felt more isolated and lonely than ever before. There was nobody to turn to, no place where she could seek refuge or protection. Ada quickly realized that the struggle for her freedom and rights had come to an end before it had even started. Within a relatively short time, she had moved from being a happy girl in a protective, loving family to an unwanted outcast without a home.

On the one hand, she considered the threat of losing her family and the unimaginable consequences of that to be real and frightening. On the other hand, the possibility of a forced marriage to an older stranger had become no less real but more scary to her, offering as it did the uncertainty of living a life in bondage. Caught between the devil and the deep blue sea with nowhere to hide or run to, Ada accepted that she had lost the fight. The best option – the only option, it now seemed to her despairing mind – was to try to please the wishes of her parents.

She spent a few days reflecting on what had happened, what could have happened, and what might happen in the future. She decided she would agree to meet this stranger to whom her parents had arranged her to marry. She would check out his background and try to extract assurances from him that he would allow her to achieve her ambition to become a lawyer. Eventually she called her parents and shared her decision with them. Her delighted mother and father hugged her with relief and reassured her that all would be well.

3

Meeting Bello

The family was once more warm, united and loving towards Ada, but deep down she was fearful of the unknown. When she was finally introduced to her proposed husband Bello, however, she was surprised and relieved that her worst fear did not materialize. Bello was not a scruffy old man and the age gap between them was not as significant as she had expected. Although he was of northern extraction and a Muslim, Bello had lived and worked for many years in the eastern part of Nigeria and had acclimatized and assimilated well with life in that area. His religion was a source of concern for Ada, but he allayed her fears with assurances that this would not create difficulties or have any prejudicial effect on their relationship because he did not take it very seriously.

Ada thought Bello to be softly spoken and modern in his attitude, behaviour and outlook. Far more significant for her was the fact that he was attractive and well educated – far beyond the level of those who had tormented her in her own family. He had a first-class degree in chemical engineering from a London university and worked as a project manager for an oil-servicing company. This gave Ada some degree of comfort and confidence in many ways. The fact that both of them had a common interest in education and were academically gifted was a plus for her, because she felt it would create a healthy, enabling environment for both of them to engage themselves in high-level intellectual discussions. Accordingly, Ada genuinely held the view that it might in fact be possible to convince him to fund and support her agenda for further education. Bello also had experience of life on two continents, because he was born and brought up in Nigeria but educated in England. Surely, she thought, that ought to be sufficient to equip him to adjust and modernize his behaviour, attitudes and general outlook on life. She hoped that Bello had duly modified his views on how Nigerian society perceived women in terms of their freedom, rights, privileges, roles, responsibilities and mode of dress. Ada found herself concluding that Bello ticked all the essential boxes and even came to believe that she could grow in time to fall in love with him.

Bello began to visit her regularly, showering her with flowers and gifts beyond her wildest dreams. Although Ada was very popular and highly sociable within her own comfort zone and in a crowd, she tended to feel very uncomfortable alone with any man. Still a virgin, she also refused several invitations from Bello to return his visits. Her refusal did not act as a deterrent to Bello. Instead it became an incentive for him to exhibit extraordinary commitment and love. They became more serious with each other as the weeks passed, to the extent that Bello became very intoxicated by his love for Ada and the possibility of a life together. He knew that he had seen enough to be persuaded that the time had come to give the relationship its proper identity and status.

He felt that he must now share his happiness with his parents, who had pestered him ever since his graduation to get married and give them grandsons. After agreeing with Ada that they should take their relationship to the next level, Bello decided to make an impromptu visit to his parents. But Ada was worried that differences of both tribe and religion were still live issues, carrying the potential to derail their plans. She asked Bello what might happen if his parents objected to their marriage. Bello assured her that he was more than capable of handling the problem because he possessed all the aces: for example, he was the only son and his parents had been waiting for the day he would settle down and begin to give them grandchildren. In any event, he added that he was merely minded to run the plan past his parents as a matter of courtesy and to fulfil the traditional protocol. He did not intend that they should have the final say.

Bello departed to his home town that weekend, determined to surprise his parents who had become accustomed to him not returning home often due to his busy work schedule. His parents were happy to see him, but had a feeling that all was not well as it was out of character for Bello to return home without notice. He told them that his engagements for the weekend had been cancelled at the last minute, which had granted him the window of opportunity to travel. Later that evening he announced that he had met the girl of his dreams and that in no time he intended to set the wedding bells ringing. His parents were delirious with joy that he had finally made the decision to marry.

The initial euphoria and excitement vanished, however, when Bello revealed that Ada originated from eastern

Nigeria. His choice of Ada and her tribe provoked strong objections and was greeted with condemnation and uncontrollable anger by his father. Bello was astonished. He had never witnessed such a reaction from his father before, and he had never thought his father capable of such a level of hatred for a fellow human being. Speechless, Bello watched his father at close range ranting and raving continuously for about fifteen minutes, with sweat streaming down his face like rainwater. Bello was eventually led away to the safety of his room by his mother, in an attempt to defuse the situation and allow his father to calm himself down.

Father and son met again the following morning, rather more calmly, and Bello was curious to know the source of his father's anger. His father told him bluntly that the cultural and religious differences between the tribes would make the marriage unworkable. This fact was compounded by the age-old mistrust between the two tribes, exacerbated by the events leading up to the Nigerian civil war. Bello could not understand what the fuss was all about: his father knew very well that he had never been serious about religion, that he had been away from home for a long time, and that his culture did not play a significant role in his life. He therefore did not see how events that had happened before he was born could seriously affect his personal life.

Bello told his father that he saw marriage as being rather like sailing through choppy and uncharted waters to an unknown destination. It was full of obstacles, dangers and both good and bad memories. The couple would carry the trials, tribulations, joy and happiness, burdens, liabilities and responsibilities associated with the marriage for the rest their lives. Other people outside the marriage (including parents) could only share their worries, sympathize or imagine the fallout of bad times but only the couple themselves would carry their cross for the rest of their lives. Therefore the choice of who should be his wife and where she should come from ought to be exclusively his own prerogative. That right and any attached privileges should be unfettered and must not be interfered with. He told his father that his aim was to remain happy in marriage, and he pleaded with his parents to allow him to be his own boss with the right to manage his own destiny and life. Finally, he warned them that if his wish was not respected, they should not expect him to return home again with any children he and Ada should produce. His father replied ominously that Ada would never be allowed to return to his compound as a daughter-in-law in his lifetime.

Bello returned to his base confident that his parents could not sustain their objection for long, because they were fully aware that they could no longer make any meaningful contribution at this late stage in his life. In fact, he claimed that they needed him more than he needed them: they could not afford to lose him. He was well aware that his parents were desperately in need of grandchildren and would do anything to achieve that goal. Armed with this weapon, he enlisted the services of some powerful and influential close family members, friends and other associates to apply pressure on his parents, particularly his father.

Happily for Bello, the tactic paid off. After some months of intense lobbying and wheeling and dealing, his parents buckled and consented to his wish to marry Ada. He shared the good news with Ada and her parents, then returned to visit his own parents to try to normalize the strained relationship. He used the opportunity to reassure them that he was doing the right thing and that Ada was the right choice for him. He added that marrying Ada might eventually help change perceptions and negative views, eliminating long-held tribal prejudices. Bello promised to inform his parents of the traditional wedding date as soon as he had agreed that date with Ada's parents.

4

A Traditional Wedding

Bello was joyous that he had finally succeeded in persuading his parents to change their views about Ada. He wasted no time in scheduling a meeting with Ada and her parents, urging them to decide on the wedding date and set in motion the preparation and completion of all the preliminary traditional activities. He reminded them that the last remaining obstacle had been removed, and therefore everything should be expedited to avoid delays and to make sure his parents had no time to introduce further challenges in order to frustrate his plans to marry Ada. Bello reiterated his promise to write off all family debts owed to him and to return all family land he held as collateral for those debts. Feeling over-excited and jubilant, Ada's father rushed to break the news to the family chief, who hastily convened a meeting of the elders. They swiftly decided on a date and handed down a pre-prepared 'customary marriage' list (of things to do and/or buy) in accordance with the tradition.

The setting of the date jumpstarted a series of coordinated activities by both parties in their joint efforts and determination to put on a well-organized traditional wedding. Bello was given a copy of the customary marriage list and informed of certain traditional 'must-do activities' which were usually completed by the groom's family before the wedding day. These activities were so important, delicate, problematic and cumbersome that they required the parties to exhibit a great deal of diplomacy and tactical sensitivity in order to reach a harmonized agreement. The essential activities included the agreement of the dowry (bride price). In traditional marriages, the mother of the bride, her father and the men and married women are the key players, and this was the case here with the Okafor family. Each has a customary marriage list that contains a number of pre-determined items that Bello must buy or accomplish before the date of the wedding. They range from shoes, watches, jewellery and native wrappers (traditional clothing) to cartons of beer and soft drink and food items, to name but a few. The bride's family usually exaggerates the numbers of each item, which then becomes the subject of negotiation between the parties. But it must not go below the minimum on each item and it must be complete otherwise there would be no marriage. This is why both parties get this part completed well on time so that the wedding on the day becomes a mere formality. It is usually easier if the bride and groom are of the same tribe because the lists are often the same, but challenges would occur if they are of different tribes. In Ada's case, the families worked admirably hard to reach an agreement on all the various points well in advance. Then they were able to move on to the next stage, commissioning a professional caterer, arranging for the supply of drinks and sending out invitations to family, friends, well-wishers, acquaintances and work colleagues.

The traditional wedding ceremony itself was described

by one journalist as a 'show-stopper', because the entire neighbourhood came to a grinding halt. The wedding was held at Ada's family home in accordance with tradition. It had all the razzmatazz and spectacle of a typical Nollywood (the Nigerian movie industry) event – colour, entertainment, pageantry, panache, beauty and fashion. It was the perfect opportunity for the audience to showcase and celebrate the creativity, innovation, luxury, style and uniqueness in native fashion in both dress and jewellery. Above all, authority was added to the occasion by the attendance and presence of family members, friends, well-wishers and the wider community in symbolic recognition of the marriage.

The DJ, a popular professional comedian who also doubled as the Master of Ceremonies for the day, set the atmosphere ablaze with popular local music and rib-cracking jokes. The decoration of the venue was lavish. Together, it all served to raise the bar of public expectation of what was to come, as well as raising the roof of the stage and encouraging the crowd into a celebratory mood.

Ada looked extraordinarily beautiful in her handmade traditional attire. She was decorated with necklaces and a hat made from rare and expensive beads that had been handed down by her great-great-grandmother and had been used by generations of women from her family during traditional weddings. Her well-manicured toe- and fingernails were complemented by her hairstyle and make-up, suggesting a professional perfection. Ada made a grand entry supported by a select group of beautiful young women, and together they displayed an impressive dance routine so carefully and meticulously choreographed that it left the audience screaming for more.

One of the highlights – a most important and much-awaited aspect of the occasion – came when Ada collected from her father a wine cup filled with highly valued local palm wine and set off in search of her husband amongst the huge crowd. Excitement reached a crescendo and the move triggered a wild interest amongst the young men as they offered themselves and pleaded (in jest) to be her worthy husband. To their theatrical disappointment, Ada rejected all of them in favour of her man. Meanwhile, other young men, mainly the groom's friends, shielded Bello from her view, but despite their concerted efforts Ada eventually found her man and walked gracefully hand-in-hand with him to show her father. Deafening, rapturous applause came from the crowd in appreciation that Ada had successfully found her husband. The couple were given the blessing and approval of Ada's father before sharing a cup of palm wine as a symbol of unity as husband and wife. Again, this was applauded by the audience in acknowledgement that they had witnessed this important aspect of the marriage ceremony.

Another significant part of the ceremony saw the bride and groom dance together in full view of the audience. This was followed by lavish food and drink, music, and the presentation of souvenirs and gifts to the newly married couple by both families, family members, friends and well-wishers. At the end, all the married women from Ada's side of the family selected a handful of women to escort Ada to her new home as a married woman.

When asked by a journalist whether she had experienced a wonderful day, Ada replied, 'I feel a sense of pride and fulfilment; it's every woman's dream to marry and leave her family home for her husband's. I would not swap today for anything in the world. My happiness knows no bounds and my affection no limits, for today is the best day of my life.'

Deep down, Ada knew that the fight for liberation, freedom, choice or control over her life had been lost. At the same time, however, she celebrated her marriage as a significant achievement and success for herself. Ada was convinced at that point that her marriage had permanently removed a destructive weapon that was often used by her society to oppress, stigmatize and victimize women. Women who are not married are sadly treated as second-class citizens and denied certain basic rights in some quarters of society. If these women chose to have children outside marriage, those innocent children were regarded as bastards and subjected to marginalization, discrimination and deprivation of rights and privileges. Although her marriage was arranged, Ada felt liberated to a certain extent because the threat of remaining unmarried, with its associated hazards, had been removed.

Her father was understandably filled with a sense of pride, joy and happiness that Ada had married during his lifetime, and he was extremely honoured to have given her hand away in marriage. To the community and the wider society, which always regarded marriage as an important institution, this marriage was a clear message to everyone: Ada was henceforth to be accorded every right and privilege exclusively reserved for married women. Furthermore, she was now protected from any act designed to induce her to engage in adultery or other immoral sexual activity. Any advance or assault on her of that nature made by anyone not her husband was regarded as taboo and a serious offence.

5

Bittersweet Home

Ada and Bello returned to their married home after the wedding feeling both physically and mentally exhausted, but joyful that all the planning had been worth it. They jetted off the next morning to an exotic destination for a well-deserved two-week honeymoon. There they had the time, space and privacy to reflect on recent events as well as on their future lives together. They discussed goals, plans and expectations which they hoped would make for a successful marriage. Generally, both expected to have a warm, loving and happy home: they recognized their duty to respect each other, and to assist each other in performing their traditional roles at home. Bello revealed his wish to have five children – four boys and a girl. With a lot of disposable income, Bello reckoned that he would have enough money to make adequate savings, acquire luxuries and afford a high-quality standard of care and education for those children, and still have enough to make decent investments in real estate for the future.

He explained to Ada that his mega-ambition was heavily influenced by his childhood and teenage experiences, which had debilitating psychological and emotional effects on him. As the first of four children, Bello had witnessed the loss of his three other siblings by the time he was ten years old. Left with no other sibling and with working-class parents who devoted much of their time to their jobs, Bello was left feeling very lonely and isolated and would often cry himself to sleep. Although his parents had a housemaid and a *megad* (security man), both of these employees were adults and too old for Bello to play or share his thoughts with. His situation was made worse by his father, who constantly reminded him that he was the only child and that he should refrain from any activities that might expose him to death or serious injury. Bello's parents were very paranoid about his personal safety, to the extent that they would not let him leave the house or make journeys unless it was absolutely necessary. Equally, they would not travel together as a family, fearing that any fatal accident could bring total extinction of the family name and lineage. And from the moment he became an adult, Bello was under immense pressure from his parents to marry and have many children to ensure the survival of the family name. Bello was therefore mindful not to let his children suffer the same experiences.

His ambitious plan to have five children was alarming to Ada, and left her feeling psychologically and emotionally paralysed as she contemplated the implications of her husband's ideals for her own ambition of acquiring a university education and becoming a professional working mother. Ada feared that her husband's plan had been made selfishly, without full consideration of her own interests, and meant a virtual house arrest for her, condemning her to life as a full-time housewife.

Furthermore, she feared that Bello might be pressured

by his parents to start having children as soon as possible. By her panicked calculations, at best she would be giving birth to those children right up to her late twenties, if not beyond. Meanwhile, her former schoolmates would be completing their university education and national youth service and might well have started finding jobs and moving on.

Faced with the very real prospect of being forced to sacrifice her own ambitions, Ada tipped over into a depressive mood and confronted Bello angrily with the challenge: was he now intending to breach his previous promise to help her further her education? Bello immediately realized that discussing the issue during their honeymoon was perhaps not the best idea – and he quickly veered away from the subject, promising to deal with Ada's concerns at a more convenient time after they had returned home.

The couple headed home at the end of their honeymoon feeling refreshed and energized after the hectic wedding period. Bello settled back into his usual work routine, while Ada began her new life as a married woman. As the weeks passed, however, Ada began to feel lonely and bored the moment her husband left for work or travelled. Then she woke up one morning to prepare breakfast for her husband as usual, but soon realized that she was feeling unwell. Bello cuddled her and persuaded her to go back to bed and get some rest.

Ada felt better as the day progressed, but the symptoms persisted the following day, with frequent vomiting. Bello decided to take Ada to the family doctor on his way to work – and the doctor later confirmed that Ada was two weeks pregnant. Despite her previous misgivings, the news brought Ada a sense of relief, excitement, happiness and tears of joy. After she had time to calm down, she asked the doctor to let her have the honour of divulging the good news to her husband. Bello was over the moon. He went out the following day and purchased a luxury Mercedes Benz as a gift for Ada.

In the following weeks and months, he pampered Ada: he showered her with flowers and expensive gifts, and generally helped with the domestic work in ways beyond her expectations. Ada felt so loved and comfortable at home during this time that she began to feel guilty for her earlier decision to question, fight and resist the whole idea of arranged marriage and her parents' choice of Bello for her. As well as being so loving, caring and helpful towards her, Bello spent quality time with her at home and took her out to functions, dinner, the cinema and shopping. Also, he made a point of returning home straight from work and resisted the temptation to hang out with friends or work colleagues in the evenings.

Meanwhile, Ada's parents were very happy that everything had worked out according to their plans. Ada was now married to the man they had arranged for her and Bello fulfilled his pre-marriage promises to write off the family's debt and to return the land which had been used as collateral. Ada's family were now liberated from all their financial encumbrances and were free to focus their attention on providing for the boys and securing their future. For her part, Ada believed that she had now repaid her family for the sacrifices they had made in providing her basic education, and she was also convinced that she was in a loving marriage with her dream man which she hoped would last forever.

In her private moments, however, Ada still reflected on the pregnancy with a mixed bag of joy, relief and fear. The pregnancy certainly signified an important victory for Ada, as society expected every married woman to bear children for her husband. Any failure to have children, irrespective of the causes, was frowned on without sympathy with mothers-in-law acting as the chief tormentors. Some women's inability to have children was one of the many weapons used by society to justify the stigmatization, marginalization, oppression and abuse of women – physically and psychologically. If a married woman had no child by the time her husband passed way, his family members would attempt to reclaim his estate in the name of tradition, using any means at their disposal, even death threats. Their success would leave the widow with little or nothing – regardless of her contributions to the creation of her husband's wealth. Ada was only too aware of the dangers involved. As far as she was concerned, therefore, her pregnancy was a step in the right direction towards security, and the birth of the child would guarantee her immunity from persecution by both her mother-in-law and the wider society.

She was also aware that it would please Bello and his parents because of their anxious desire to keep the family name alive. Furthermore, she knew that childlessness was often one of the oppressive tools used by husbands and their supporters to justify any decision to chase a wife out of her married home, to send her back to her parents, to abuse her physically or mentally, to deny her the rights accorded to wives and mothers, or to justify the husband marrying a second wife. When the child was born, therefore, Ada would be sufficiently protected from all those dangers of abuse at the hands of her husband and his parents.

At the other end of the spectrum, the downside of the pregnancy for Ada was that it was only the first step in Bello's plan to have five children. She was facing a long road. Ada contemplated the responsibility and burden of having five children and caring for a large family at her young age. But she was quick to accept that becoming a full-time housewife was her only option – for now. At least the period of this, her first pregnancy, was full of undiluted love, attention, care and happiness, which she hoped would remain permanently inscribed in her heart regardless of what might happen to the relationship in future.

The arrival of Ada's first child, Amina, eleven months after her wedding ushered in another period of joy and unforgettable memories. In addition to unwavering support and care from Bello, Ada experienced unprecedented offers of help and support from both her own parents and Bello's parents. In accordance with tradition, Ada's mother and mother-in-law took turns to assist her as soon as Amina was born, with each staying at least three months. Ada therefore enjoyed six months of pampering, grooming and being cared for like a queen by two experienced older mothers – who would not let her touch Amina except for moments of bonding or breastfeeding. Events before and after the birth of Amina led Ada to predict that she would be a special girl in the future.

Ada's father and father-in-law visited on various occasions when their respective wives were with Ada. Both seemed genuinely very happy for the birth of Amina, but deep down they both knew that they would have preferred the birth of a male child first. The bottom line for them, however, was that Ada had passed the first test of proving that she could successfully bear children. Time would tell whether Ada was capable of passing the ultimate test of producing male children.

But Bello's father was unequivocal about his views during a private conversation with his son. He was well aware that Bello possessed a nonchalant view of his culture and traditions. More worrisome for his father was the fact that Bello did not seem to understand the traditional implications of not having a male child in the family. His father took the view that Bello must now be made to understand the expectations regarding male children. So he tried, during this meeting with his son, to itemize the reasons and expectations in graphic detail. He warned Bello about the risk of losing everything, including the family name and lineage, if they all died without a grandson from him. The only beneficiaries in such a case would be their more distant relations, who would inherit the family estate. Female children could not rescue the situation because they were precluded from inheriting by tradition, due to the presumption that they would marry and join their husbands' homes and families. He therefore demanded grandsons as soon as possible and urged Bello to do everything he could towards realizing that urgent need.

This provoked anger from Bello, who protested very strongly against his father's attempt to impose his will on himself and his wife, thereby placing unfair and unbearable pressure on them. He told his father that his adopted Western values were totally in conflict with some of the native values and beliefs – which he considered to be anachronistic and as out of date as the dinosaurs. He would not allow himself, he said, to be enslaved by values and beliefs that were so irrelevant and inconsistent with the realities of the modern world. Did his father not recognize that they were all part of a global village now, a world increasingly driven by information and computer technology?

In an impassioned speech, Bello invited his father to liberate himself from the shackles of old values that had imprisoned generations of men and women, and allow himself to enter the modern world so that he could enjoy the benefits of exposure to other people, other cultures, customs and traditions. He would be able to look externally to identify good ideas and practices from other cultures in other countries, importing suitable ideas to complement the good local customary practices. At the same time he would be able to look internally to identify and jettison any obstructive and obsolete ideas, values and practices that had impeded social development in Nigeria for centuries. He reminded his father that producing children had always been the will of God through a biological process, and that the determination of the sex of any child falls only within God's superior knowledge, power and control. Finally, Bello told his father that male children would come when the time was right, but if it pleased God not to give him male children, so be it.

His father expressed total disappointment in his son's 'illogical and insensitive' observations and pronouncements. Bello was shocked to hear his father accuse him of being brainwashed, mentally enslaved, emotionally besieged and psychologically colonized by Western values – a culture he described as morally bankrupt and hopelessly deficient in some aspects. His father was particularly dismayed that a first-class brain like Bello's apparently lacked the capability to comprehend and distinguish between the most basic things that demarcated the two societies, which set them apart and made them function differently. He highlighted the differences in family set-up, in the operations of land law in the villages and towns, in the need and expectation to own the family home and be buried in ancestral villages, to say nothing of other religious and cultural differences. These marked differences, his father argued, were the key determinants that defined the way each society operated.

Although he conceded that Bello was lacking a detailed knowledge of his own culture and tradition due to long periods away from home, and as a result seemed to be stranded in a 'cultural desert', he charged his son with the task of 'de-colonizing' himself as a matter of urgency. Bello, he said, needed to be released from the 'contamination' of Western values and to gain a proper understanding of his native culture, rather than simply being dismissive of traditional values on the strength of ignorance.

The encounter with his father was acrimonious and unpleasant for Bello, but it did not affect his thinking or change his mind on the main issues; nor did it derail his affection for and commitment to Ada and his daughter. Instead, he became an even more committed father and husband.

Ten months after Amina was born, the family doctor confirmed that Ada was expecting twins. Nine months later, Ayesha and Halima arrived. Ada was initially worried that Bello might react differently to the news of two more girls, but to her astonishment he was over the moon when he arrived at the hospital to see them. Bello returned home after the hospital visit and divulged the good news to his parents. His father replied dismissively, 'Now that you have three daughters, when will your wife give you a son? When those daughters marry and leave you for their husbands, who will live with you in your old age, inherit your estate and maintain your family name when you pass on?' He ended the conversation with an ominous warning: 'Don't call me again until you hear the voice of a male child in your house.'

Bello felt deflated, and was left speechless by what he had just heard from his father. He was fully aware that his father wanted a grandson or grandsons, but he had not realized the degree of his desperation. Bello went to the hospital four days later to bring his wife and twin daughters home, where they celebrated with their neighbours. Ada's parents visited as expected, with her mother staying to assist in accordance with tradition. Bello's mother visited soon after the birth, but left a few days later with a promise to return after three months to offer her round of assistance. Meanwhile, there was no sign of Bello's father. Bello was unsurprised, and when Ada asked about her father-in-law, he simply gave her a convenient excuse.

Bello's nightmare started soon after his mother returned to assist Ada in accordance with tradition. Starting from where her husband had left off on the last occasion, she tried her best to persuade him to understand why he must have male children, why Ada would never give him male children, and why he should therefore consider taking another wife from his village. She even revealed a secret arrangement that was already in place for him to marry 'a good girl' from his home town. Bello bullishly told her that he was not bothered about having no male children, and that he was happy and comfortable with Ada and their daughters. The pressure from his mother continued over her three-month stay, but throughout this period, Ada was unaware that her house was already burning and about to collapse on her. Bello and his mother perfected the art of masking their anger and frustration at one another without Ada noticing what was going on under her roof.

Peace and tranquillity only returned for Bello after the departure of his mother. He wrestled with the urge to tell Ada what had been eating him up during her stay, but in the end resisted the temptation on the basis that it might cause more damage in the long run. The family remained happy and loving. Bello enjoyed a promotion at work, which meant increased pay and perks. He returned home early as often as he could to assist Ada and to play with his children. The good atmosphere was crowned with the news that Ada was pregnant for the third time, just eleven months after the birth of the twins. The couple prayed and asked God to give them a male child so that they could put a stop to having children and concentrate instead on bringing them up.

Unfortunately, Ada had a very difficult pregnancy this time around, which required several hospital visits. After eight and a half months, Ada had another baby girl, Zennab, by caesarean section. The operation caused serious complications which prompted the doctors to advise Ada that she would never be pregnant again. This devastating news came at the worst possible time for the couple. It was a cul-de-sac as far as their chances of male children were concerned. For Bello, the bad news did not trouble him unduly, but he was deeply concerned that it would present a perfect opportunity for his parents to instigate another wave of pressure and torment.

Regrettably, Ada's mother could not assist her daughter this time, as she was suffering a recurrence of a serious long-term illness. This left the coast clear for Bello's mother to assist Ada for a period of six months. Bello knew that it would be six months of hell. Facing a dilemma, Bello carefully considered all his options. If he refused his mother's help, he must find a convincing reason to justify his decision, especially as she had assisted on previous occasions and was apparently willing and able to come this time also. The second option was to hire a housemaid, but again, how would he justify this decision to Ada without revealing the wrangling that had been going on behind the scenes? She would be puzzled at the very least, since his mother would render the help free of charge. After long deliberation, Bello opted to allow his mother to come, because he felt that the risk of not allowing her to come was greater.

His mother arrived, and the first three weeks passed without any unpleasant incidents – much to the relief of Bello, who naively started to count his chickens. During the fourth week, his mother demanded to know what his plans were, now that Ada had been advised by the doctors that she would never be pregnant again.

Bello was shocked. Unaware of his mother's hidden intentions, Ada had clearly let the cat out of the bag. He told his mother that he intended to do nothing, because the children he already had were enough and he now wished to focus his attention on caring and providing for them. This provoked a serious tongue-lashing from his mother, who compared him to friends, cousins and age mates in his home town who had two, three or four male children each. She repeated her previous observations on why he must have male children at all costs. She finally threatened to bring a wife for him from his home town, if he himself did not find a wife who would produce male children for him within the next six months. After six months, following a stay marred by continuous arguments and tension, Bello's mother left his home leaving him in no doubt about what she and her husband proposed to do about his and Ada's situation.

The complex and uncomfortable situation at home was magnified by Bello's work colleagues and friends who regularly came to work with news about the birth of baby boys by their wives or the wives of people close to them. They also made jokes which Bello sadly found tasteless and which seemed to him like mockery aimed at his four daughters: 'My son will marry your first daughter!' or 'I will soon come to your house to formally betroth my son to one of your daughters' or 'We are looking for a wife for my nephew' or 'My son is engaged to Amina'. In the ordinary course of events, such harmless banter was common between friends and colleagues, and the intention was generally to amuse rather than cause offence. But in Bello's case, the unhealthy atmosphere prevailing at his home clouded his thinking and left him unable to process such comments as the harmless jokes they were. Instead, he quickly linked them up with what his parents were preaching to him about male children.

Furthermore, in his desperation to seek help and to offload some of the worries from his chest, Bello inadvertently ended up amplifying the pressure on himself.

He enlisted the help of a tried and tested friend, Femi, and hastily arranged to meet up so that he could discuss his problems with him. During their meeting, Bello professed his love for Ada, laid bare his parents' concerns, revealed his fear that Ada might not now give him any male children, and finally confessed that he was in a confused state of mind which had paralysed his ability to fashion a way forward.

Femi expressed concern that Bello should need to be told by his parents or anyone else about the role and importance of men in their society and the need to have a least one male child. He said that he was a proud father of four sons and a daughter and that he expected his daughter to marry and leave home one day, with the boys left to perform the customary roles in the family – just as it had all been explained by Bello's father in the past. Echoing Bello's father, he asked, 'Who is going to look after you when you are old? Who will maintain your name, lineage and your legacy long after you have died?' Femi went on to encourage Bello to 'wake-up' from his slumber and activate plans to have male children as quickly as possible, since it had been confirmed that Ada would never produce male children for him. He advised that getting a mistress or a second wife straight away were the only viable options open to him.

For Bello, that meeting with his trusted friend and confidant was a game-changer. It added another layer of complications with far-reaching repercussions to an already complex situation. The views expressed by Femi, taken together with previous advice and comments from his parents and colleagues, started to weaken the strong views he had held on the issue up until then. He found himself beginning to appreciate some of the underlying logic behind his parents' views. He had a hard choice to make. Should he stay with Ada and his daughters, or should he take a second wife and try for male children? Either way, he knew that the consequences would be painful, bruising and challenging for all concerned, and life as they knew it would not be the same again.

He considered his options very carefully. His first option, of course, was to stay with Ada and his daughters. This would mean that he might never have male children, or associated traditional benefits which they would bring. Also he would inevitably expose himself to the risk of abuse, mockery, alienation and sustained pressure from his parents, friends and the wider society. On the flip side, he and his family would be happy, and he would be able to concentrate on his duty to provide for them.

If, on the other hand, he elected to take a second wife, he would increase the chances of having male children, which would be greeted with joy by his parents and friends, and would bring him all the benefits that come with having male children. On the down side, this course of action would bring hurt and pain to Ada and her children. It could also bring Bello himself much unhappiness, in the form of unnecessary distraction, divided attention and love, the need to duplicate resources, and inevitable rivalry and jealousy.

Eventually, after much deep thought, Bello opted to take a second wife. The next massive challenge for him was how best to communicate his decision to Ada. How was he to do this? How could he minimize the distress and pain she would certainly feel at such a betrayal?

A few weeks after Bello's mother had left, the atmosphere at home was still normal, except that the couple had more domestic work to do without the extra pair of hands. Bello, as always, combined his office duties with his domestic work extremely well. Nonetheless, he was troubled and preoccupied with what he was about to do, worried about the effect on Ada and the children and how it might all work out. At times he felt pity for them as innocent victims of his own selfishness and self-centredness, driven by tradition and his parents' obsession for male children. Bello spent several months battling with self-criticism, re-evaluating the alternatives and planning how best to mitigate the effects of his decision.

One evening after work, his colleagues suggested a group get-together to socialize. Bello was reluctant at first, but then agreed because he did not want to be seen as anti-social. He also thought that it would be a temporary getaway from a life dominated by worries and self-pity. It was a perfect opportunity to drop his guard, to wind down and to release the stress.

In breach of the high standards and expectations he normally set for himself, he failed to make the usual courtesy call to Ada and the children to say hello and to let her know that he might return home late. His experiences that evening were an eye-opener for him, reminding him that there was much excitement, enjoyment and satisfaction to be found outside the married home. The lively, liberating atmosphere made him crave for more. He eventually returned home very late. Sensing behaviour that was out of character for her husband, Ada asked if all was well and why he had returned so late. Bello simply pleaded forgetfulness due to work pressure and rendered an apology, all in the same breath. Ada quickly smelled a rat and felt suspicious that things were somehow not quite adding up, but she decided not to pursue the matter further just then as Bello already seemed in an agitated mood.

The following morning he left home without the usual goodbye kiss. Again, he returned very late in the evening – but this time Ada smelled alcohol on his breath. It was very late on a Thursday evening, however, and Ada felt that it was a good idea to leave matters until the weekend. Her husband had dinner after his shower and then, going into the bedroom, proceeded to demand sex with a touch of aggression. Ada declined his approach, on the grounds that she was still breast feeding and in any event it was not safe. While her husband slept, Ada reflected on his unusual behaviour over the previous few days: he was acting quite outside his normal character. She was suddenly convinced that something huge was about to happen that would rock her marriage, but she could not yet put her finger on anything specific. She prayed that God should take control.

After dinner on the Friday evening, Ada demanded to know what had been eating him up in the past few days. Bello initially tried to wave off her concern with flimsy work-related excuses. He was flabbergasted and embarrassed when Ada asked him straight out: 'Has the spark gone out of our marriage because I can't give you a male child?'

Looking very subdued, Bello quietly admitted that the issue had been troubling him ever since the doctors had advised against having more children. He added that he had been at war with his parents, who had pestered him to give them grandsons. He further claimed that they had mocked him endlessly and threatened to find another wife for him to marry but that he had always resisted and fought for her corner.

Clearly disturbed and distressed about what she was hearing, Ada asked, 'How long has this been going on?'

He replied, 'Since the birth of our first daughter and every subsequent visit my mother has made – including the recent one.'

Ada was further told that her father-in-law refused to attend the births of their children after Amina because they were not male. Ada asked: 'All this has been happening under my roof and you kept it to yourself, why?'

Bello insisted that he wasn't bothered by it at the time and so did not feel it was necessary to tell her. He also added that it would have caused more problems in the relationship.

Ada asked, 'What are you going to do about it now?'

He said that the pressure was becoming unbearable both physically and mentally and that his parents were determined to bring a wife to him. He went on to add that he had made up his mind to take a second wife in the interests of the family. Ada immediately erupted into uncontrolled anger. Her husband had crossed a line. The news occasioned a horrified Ada to display a beast she did not even realize was inside her. The couple engaged in a long, heated argument, with Ada unleashing so much fury that Bello wondered if she was possessed by some alien monster. He was powerless to stop her as she screamed, hit and scratched him with her long fingernails, threw objects at him, and caused a significant amount of damage around the house. Eventually, when she had calmed down out of sheer exhaustion, Ada pleaded with her husband to consider other alternatives.

At this troubling, testing and most vulnerable time, Ada was ready to listen to any advice that might offer a solution to her urgent problem. The first idea was to start an emotional and psychological war by accusing him of betrayal, abuse, exploitation, abandonment, insensitivity and immorality. In particular, he was accused of abusing and exploiting her parents' state of vulnerability at a time of extreme poverty and financial difficulties, in that he deceived and coerced them to agree to his proposal to marry her with a promise to write off debts owed to him.

Ada also accused him of abandonment and betrayal now that he had achieved his aim. Bello was further accused of conspiring and colluding with his parents to victimize her for not producing male children and for marginalizing her and her daughters on the basis of their gender. Ada finally threatened to end her life in a suicide pact with the children if he went ahead to marry a second wife. But her effort was like water off a duck's back as her emotional ploy did not have any positive effect on her husband, who remained entrenched in his bunker.

In her desperation, Ada naively turned to a few family friends and neighbours for help. This opened the way to a flood of suggestions from a multitude of people. Suddenly Ada realized that her problem was quite prevalent in the community, but while everyone seemed to have similar problems, they all offered different solutions. Ada was ready to try anything, regardless of how bizarre, illogical or ridiculous it might seem. Even Bello, usually so sceptical and suspicious when it came to native culture and customs, was sucked in as he jettisoned his so-called Western values and mentality in his quest to find an alternative solution to what was clearly a medical problem.

So, under the influence of some illiterate community members, this exceptionally brilliant and well-educated couple were led to believe that their problem was not medical but an unmistakable 'spiritual attack'. Consequently they allowed themselves to be dragged from one *dibia* to another and from one *juju* shrine to another in search of a solution to their problem. The *dibias* and *juju* priests blamed jealous neighbours, work colleagues, friends and family members, their ancestors and the gods for their problem. The couple covered thousands of miles in journeys to these practitioners, spent a fortune and were expected to make all kinds of sacrifices but all to no avail. It only dawned on them that all this demanding ritual as nothing but an elaborate scam when they were asked at one of the *juju* shrines to bring human parts and a large sum of money for sacrifice. It was at this juncture that they suddenly realized they were chasing a mirage. By this stage, however, the damage had been done: they had already isolated many family members, friends, colleagues and neighbours as 'enemies' on the false understanding that these individuals were somehow responsible for their problem.

Shortly after their ordeal with the *dibias* and *juju* priests, offers of help flooded in from Pentecostal churches professing to be able to deliver the couple from their predicament. With limited options left, Ada yet again successfully persuaded her husband to seek divine help. The couple visited many churches, prayer houses, pastors and prophets, and found themselves engaged in various fasting sessions, prayer sessions, night vigils and miracle healing crusades.

When every attempt had failed, Ada moved on to encourage her husband to consider the adoption of a male child as a genuine final option. This, she argued, would achieve the same as having a biologically related male child, and would avoid the need of a second wife and therefore eliminate the dangers associated with running two families and managing two wives.

Bello swiftly ruled out adoption as a viable alternative, because for him it meant taking another man's son – albeit legally. Apart from the well-documented risks associated with adoption, he strongly maintained that adoption would not resolve the fundamental problem of blood lineage. He explained the whole thing to Ada at some length and in great detail.

In accordance with tradition, the key issue for him was to have a male son who would be of his own flesh and blood, and would assume the responsibility to maintain the family lineage and legacy long after Bello had passed away. He argued that this was what would provide the incentive and the enabling environment to nurture, care and love the child unconditionally. In addition, as far as Bello himself was concerned, there were no medical or biological reasons for him not to have his own blood son. Adoption, on the other hand, meant taking another man's son, which would fail to address the issue of lineage and as a result might be a barrier to unconditional love, care and bonding. This would not be good for the adopted child's development and general welfare in the long run.

Equally significant for Bello was the fear that the couple might automatically become a kind of amusement park in their community if they decided to adopt a male child. This, he said, was a very sceptical and suspicious society where adoption enjoyed very limited acceptance and carried a high degree of stigma. Bello had no doubt that he and Ada would instantly become objects of caricature to his parents, friends and the men and women in their neighbourhood. Mockery, ridicule, gossip, vicious rumours and hurtful comments would be rife. Adoption would expose them to the suspicion that they had deep-rooted biological or medical problems, or that they had offended the traditional gods, or that they practised witchcraft or were members of a cult and had sacrificed their male children. Bello feared that he would be regarded as 'not man enough' to produce male children of his own, opting instead for the easy route of adopting another man's son. Ada would be accused and tormented by other women, led by her mother-in-law, facing accusations that she was not able to produce male children for her husband and was therefore not fit to regard herself as Bello's wife.

Bello also argued that adoption was a risky journey into the unknown in a country with exceptionally poor medical care. Adopting a child without full knowledge of the family medical history or without the facilities to conduct a full medical check on the child might be challenging. Genetic and inherited diseases such as cancer, diabetes, Parkinson's disease, Alzheimer's, sickle cell anaemia and more could pose difficulties in terms of diagnosis and treatment. In a country where the majority of its population lived in abject poverty, where genuine medicines were rendered hugely expensive with a history of fake drugs, and where the quality of medical care and facilities was limited, the costs of treating such inherited illnesses become more difficult and prohibitively expensive. These factors, he said, might create extra emotional difficulties and frustration, which would impact negatively on the relationship between the child and his adoptive parents.

Another key point for Bello was the fact that adoption agencies in Nigeria were not strictly regulated, which made the whole adoption process a favourite feeding ground for criminal gangs. Bello reckoned that there were documented cases of babies being stolen from their parents and sold on to shady agencies, who then charged desperate and vulnerable prospective adoptive parents astronomical administrative fees and other hidden costs. Years later, when the truth emerged, these adoptive parents were left to pick up the pieces and face the consequences, including possible loss of the child they had cared for, and prosecution for stealing, illegal adoption and conspiracy, as well as the loss of financial and emotional investments.

Furthermore, adoption posed additional risks to adoptive parents due to the endemic bribery and corruption in Nigeria. It had penetrated deep into the legal system and the police, Bello said. Although adoption might be genuine in the first instance, with the biological parents truly opting to give up their male child(ren) because of poverty or youth, years down the road the natural parents might wish to challenge the adoption process. The biological parents might then do everything within their powers to get their son back. They might use the corrupt legal system and the police, or threats and intimidation, adverse publicity, physical assault or even resort to murder. The adoptive parents might be subjected to many years of protracted legal cases and would live in constant fear for their safety and even their lives. If they failed in their defence of the adoption, the purpose of adopting in the first place would be defeated and they would have everything to lose, emotionally and financially.

Also, Bello was fully aware that children who had been adopted were constantly bullied. As adults they tended to suffer discrimination and victimization from those closely related to their adoptive parents – particularly when one or both parents passed away. As a result, adoptive children often went in search of their biological parents, either out of curiosity or to find out why they were given up for adoption. And if for any reason the son decided to return voluntarily to his biological parents, then the purpose of the adoption would again be defeated, with no remedy for the adoptive parents.

After such a detailed explanation of the risks pertaining to adoption, Ada was sympathetic to her husband's concerns. However, she suggested that they could consider moving to another city to avoid some of the problems that Bello had outlined. Again, he rejected the idea: the issues of lineage and the family name could not be remedied by migration or running away, he said.

Having exhausted all the avenues she could think of in search of a solution, Ada spent some time reflecting on the magnitude of the challenges ahead. She was left feeling perplexed, confused and emotionally overwhelmed. She was convinced that when fate strikes, society was only too quick to use such bad luck as a weapon against women. For the second time within a short period, Ada predicted that fate and tradition might conspire once again to cause havoc and devastation in her young life. The first incident had been her father's preference to provide education and secure the future of his male children. On that occasion, she had become the sacrificial lamb as her academic and future ambitions were summarily terminated and she was shipped out of the family at a tender age into an arranged marriage. Her family had prioritized the needs of her brothers over her own needs, even though she had come before them.

Now, just as she was making the best of the bad situation into which she had been forced, and just as things were beginning to move in the right direction, her world was about to be shattered for the second time. This time the convenient excuse was her failure to produce male children for her husband. The fact that she had produced four healthy daughters was apparently irrelevant. If and when the second wife came in and began to produce male children, Ada predicted that she and her daughters would be subjected to bitter rivalry and jealousy, discrimination, ignominy, divided attention from Bello, physical, psychological and emotional abuse, and Ada herself would be treated as second best.

Paradoxically, some couples around the world would do anything to have children irrespective of their sex – including surrogacy and IVF treatments. Ada felt that in her own case, it had always been about male children and the priority of their rights over her rights. In other developed and developing societies, most couples would have accepted gladly the four healthy girls she had laboured so painfully to produce for her husband. Why did it have to be so different in her own society?

Ada eventually came to the realization that wallowing in self-pity and sorrow and trying to play the blame game would not make her nightmare to go away. She encouraged herself to remain focused and try to devise the right strategy to deal with her troubles. Her first option was to engage the services of 'influencers' or 'persuaders' to encourage her husband to veer away from his current position. But she soon came to the conclusion that such persuaders were few and far between. The couple had led a fairly reclusive life after their marriage, keeping themselves to themselves, with communication mostly restricted to their respective parents and a trusted friend of Bello.

The first influencer for Ada was her father, the chief architect of her troubles. Her father said he understood Bello's dilemma, having had a similar experience himself during the five years after Ada was born. He added that they lived in a society and an era where a man was expected to have a male child or children for strong cultural reasons. He rehashed all the discussions they had been through regarding Ada's desire for further education and the stronger claims of her brothers due to the roles they were expected to play in the family. He also told Ada that the matter of male children had dominated his thoughts since the birth of Amina and the subsequent births of her other daughters. He had not wanted to alarm or pressure her, however, so had resisted the temptation to say anything earlier to warn her of the dangers of not producing a male child. He also confessed to having had a naive belief that Bello would not be so concerned about the lack of a male heir. However, he now advised Ada to prepare herself for the worst-case scenario, because it was within Bello's traditional rights to take a second wife and there was nothing Ada or anybody else could do to stop him.

He suggested that Ada should now adjust her expectations and attitude to help her adapt more easily to her new situation. She must do her best, he said, to promote peace and harmony with her husband and her rival, in order to extract the best deal for herself and her children. The only alternative, he warned her, was divorce – which he said was impossible and unthinkable. There were several reasons for this. If she divorced, her father would be expected to return the bride price, something which he made categorically clear to Ada that he would not do. Divorce would also leave a permanent stain and bring shame to the family and Ada'sparents. In addition, Ada and her children might suffer extreme financial hardship, because Bello might abandon her and her children without offering any financial support. They would then have no place to go except Ada's original family home, which would invariably result in overcrowding and all the associated difficulties.

Her father promised to hold a meeting with Bello in due course to discuss and suggest some alternatives, but he was not prepared to give any guarantees about the outcome. As he warned Ada, any proposal that would not guarantee her husband male children of his own was likely to be rejected.

Having heard him out, Ada looked straight into her father's face and told him that she was not surprised by what he had said. She had effectively heard it all before. She accused him of using threats and intimidation when she was just sixteen to plunge her forcefully into the situation that had led directly to her present difficulties. She recalled his threats to denounce her as a daughter, to ostracize her from the family and to refuse to give her hand in marriage to any other man except Bello. She threatened to hold her father responsible for all that had happened to her in the past and for what might happen to her and her daughters in the future.

Following the meeting with her father, Ada swiftly proceeded to speak also to her husband's parents and his trusted friend. Unfortunately, they were united in their support for Bello's decision to marry a second wife. They too hid behind the pressures of cultural expectations as a convenient excuse.

It soon became obvious to Ada that this was one fight which had no prospect of victory for her. The forces ranged against her were simply too formidable. With no help, support or even sympathy from her family and friends, options had become a luxury she could not afford. Ada was left feeling even more isolated, lonely and vulnerable than she had before.

She arranged a heart-to-heart meeting with her husband, during which she confirmed her withdrawal of her objections to his plan to take a second wife and pledged to support him. She managed to secured assurances from Bello that she and her daughters would not suffer as a result of his new wife. The couple reached agreement on several other areas, including assurances of attention and commitment for her and her daughters, the provision of adequate care and maintenance, medical care, education, security and protection from harassment and abuse. Regardless of these assurances, Ada ended the meeting feeling defeated and humiliated for being on her knees, begging and capitulating on an issue where – in a fairer world – she should rightfully be able to stand bold and tall, asserting her rights with confidence.

6

A Shared Husband

Bello duly married his second wife, Hannah, in a simple low-key ceremony and over the course of the next five years she had three sons. Although the arrival of the male children was marked with huge celebration for obvious reasons, cultural implications for both Ada and her daughters were significant. The sons, although younger than the daughters, would automatically become the chief custodians and administrators of the family on the death of their father, to the exclusion of the female children since tradition assumed that the girls would marry and leave the family home. Even in the unlikely event that the female children failed to marry, they would play little or no part in managing the family home. According to tradition, the male children had exclusive right of inheritance, so Ada's daughters would get nothing, unless their father chose to protect both Ada and her daughters in a legal will. Even the sons and other family members could still mount a successful challenge based on culture and tradition, and in extreme cases employing illegal means to oust the daughters from their inheritance. In addition, by virtue of her status as the mother of Bello's sons, Hannah automatically held pole position in the household, by implication gaining a strong advantage over Ada, even though tradition recognized Ada as the first wife.

During the first five years after the arrival of Hannah and the births of her three sons, relationships within the family were cordial, happy and respectful. Bello fulfilled his responsibilities and treated everyone fairly as he had promised. In general, Ada had no cause to complain, particularly as her husband had a well-paid job and therefore enough money to satisfy everyone's needs. There was no apparent competition and this period of their lives was particularly good and trouble free for Ada and her children. Her daughters enjoyed a head start to their education which Ada was desperate to provide. In light of her own bitter and painful experiences, she was only too anxious to see her daughters empowered through good education.

The only downside for Ada during this period was the experience of sharing the attention, love and care of her husband with another woman: Bello divided his time between them on an alternate weekly basis. Ada recalled times past when she had enjoyed the exclusive and uninterrupted monopoly of her husband's attention, with the right to warm his bed every night. All that exclusivity had now evaporated – merely because fate had denied her the opportunity to produce male children. Traditional culture was punishing her for something she could do nothing about. The emotional and psychological trauma of this situation drove her to contemplate the unthinkable on several occasions, but her children provided her always with the incentive and strength to survive those first five years of sharing her husband with another woman under the same roof.

Then the steady nature of their lives changed. The next three years ushered in what Ada described as the worst period of her life, as their living standards plummeted and everything about the family went into free fall towards abject poverty. First, Bello had some problem at work which led to his suspension for three months. After that, he lost his comfortable, well-paid job altogether. He proceeded to the courts in an attempt to get justice and to clear his name, but delays in the legal system frustrated his efforts and merely prolonged the matter with no end or benefit in sight.

Initially the family were able to cope, but the situation deteriorated with such rapidity that they had little or no time to adjust to it. Suddenly resources that had been more than enough were no longer sufficient to satisfy the ever-increasing demand of a growing family. It became necessary to introduce 'austerity measures' in order to instil discipline and encourage everyone to adjust to the new situation. Accordingly, a review of all the family expenses was conducted. Value, weight and priority were allotted to each item. Even expenses such as food and education were not ring-fenced – even there some savings would have to be made. Ada's children, for example, attended one of the most expensive private schools in the area, but a decision was made to place them in another very good but less expensive school as part of the cost-cutting exercise.

Regrettably, the dramatic changes in the family's fortune together with the introduction of these austerity measures invariably generated a lot of tension, fermenting poisonous relationships within the family, and building up violent competition and jealousy. For the next three years Ada and her daughters became sitting targets as they were subjected daily to appalling domestic abuse – including abusive and insulting words, common assault, grievous bodily harm, aggravated criminal damage and even rape in marriage, causing profound emotional and psychological abuse.

According to Ada, the second wife was the main perpetrator of the abuse which she and her daughters suffered. Hannah was a violent aggressor, a control freak, an obsessive manipulator and compulsive liar who completely dominated Bello. She used a combination of violence, fear, intimidation, threats and blackmail to get what she wanted or there would never be peace in the house. She knew that her coming in as a second wife was essentially driven by her husband's obsession to have male children. She was also aware that he derived immense joy and pride from their sons and regarded them quite simply as his 'treasure base'. Hannah successfully converted this into a source of power, control and influence for herself, manipulating things to her favour. She callously used her sons as a bargaining chip or instrument of threat in order to extract favours from her husband, often threatening to go into hiding with them or send them to her brother in the UK if she did not get what she wanted.

Ada was lucky to the extent that she was the first wife and she had produced all her children before Hannah came on the scene. This meant that her children were much older and had a headstart in most aspects – particularly in education. But the cost of their education constituted a significant part of the family budget, which became the genesis of most of the quarrels with Hannah. For three years Hannah latched on to this as an excuse to run a vicious smear campaign about Ada and her children. First, she used it to win a malicious war regarding personal allowances, which earned her a disproportionately higher personal allowance than that given to Ada. Second, Hannah waged a campaign aimed at manipulating Bello into stopping the funding for the girls' education. Hannah claimed that the family finances were being depleted at an alarming rate at a time when they were already in extremely bad shape. She urged Bello to stop wasting precious resources on educating the girls to the detriment of her boys, who would naturally become chief custodians of the family affairs long after the girls had married and left home. Hannah habitually instigated a fight at the beginning of each school term when the girls' fees were due to be paid. As a direct result of these fights, Ada sustained serious multiple injuries to the head, legs, hands and body, some of which required hospital admission for treatment.

The most difficult part for Ada and her children was the endless emotional and psychological torture perpetuated on a daily basis by Hannah. She derived great pleasure from tormenting, humiliating and embarrassing Ada or her children whenever and wherever the opportunity presented itself. Self-restraint and good manners in public meant nothing to Hannah. She was more than happy to wash the family's dirty linen in public, and she humiliated Ada in public at every opportunity, referring to her as an 'incomplete woman' because of her inability to produce male children for her husband, urging her to stop 'parading herself' as a wife, even saying Ada should contemplate suicide for her failure to produce a male child. Ada was constantly accused of being a witch who had sacrificed all her male children before they were conceived in her womb. Hannah also called her a wicked mother who had offended the gods, and accused Ada of fermenting an atmosphere of poisonous jealousy against Hannah and her sons. Hannah often teased Ada with mocking offers to let her borrow or rent one of her sons for a large fee. She took every opportunity to tell Ada's children that they had no foundation in the family, because as mere daughters they were excluded from the security provided by traditional inheritance patterns. She even warned her sons in public not to accept food or drink from Ada because she would try to kill them with poison if she could.

This horrific experience of mental torture and persistent public humiliation caused Ada to suffer chronic depression, stress, pain and anger. In particular, she felt unadulterated anger and hostility towards her parents, holding them responsible for engineering her predicament by forcing her into an arranged marriage in the first place. In addition she accused her husband of acquiescing to the abuse and encouraging such bad treatment to prevail in his own house. She railed against society for allowing such traditional beliefs to flourish, and even against fate, for denying her the opportunity to produce male children.

Her horrendous experiences at the hands of Hannah were only magnified by a preposterous accusation from Bello himself that Ada had deliberately filled his family home with female children but had failed to produce a single male child for him, thereby forcing him to marry a monster who was hell bent on making his life a living hell. Often he became so angry and frustrated that he would subject Ada to serious verbal abuse just to ventilate that anger. He also claimed to own Ada's body and her life, and started to say that he could do whatever he pleased with her. Often at a bad moment for Ada, he would approach her for sex and, if she was courageous enough to object or to make any attempt to resist him, her reward would be instant violation. Having satisfied himself, Bello would casually walk way as if nothing had happened. Ada would be left to cry herself to sleep, with only her daughters to console her.

Apart from her children's school fees, Ada experienced a massive reduction in her living standard and personal allowance as her budget was slashed far below that of her counterpart Hannah. Ada and her daughters were reduced to living like slaves in their own home. Life became more and more difficult. The deliberate starvation of funds by Bello, encouraged by Hannah, nearly suffocated Ada's will to live. Each request for an increase in allowance for her and the girls was met with resistance, endless arguments, a torrent of abuse and insulting references to the cost of the girls' school fees. For the sake of peace, Ada stopped asking – but that meant hardship.

Although the constant abuse, fights and hospitalizations were no longer news in the neighbourhood, what the neighbours frequently witnessed was sufficient to cause them to fear for the personal safety of Ada and her children. On numerous occasions neighbours encouraged Ada to return to her father's family home, albeit on a temporary basis, and Ada did indeed take heed of their advice a number of times. But these frequent returns to her father's home caused embarrassment to both her and her parents – and in any case as soon as she went back to her husband's home, the quarrels and fighting resumed. Interventions had been made by Ada's parents, her in-laws and even Hannah's family at various times in an attempt to resolve disputes, in accordance with the local custom, but to no avail. The families had made concerted attempts to address the offending behaviour without any success: an array of sanctions such as reprimands, warnings, fines and other threats to Bello and Hannah had produced no visible changes to their respective behaviour. In a last-ditch effort to find a solution to her family and personal problems, Ada was advised to seek divine help. Accordingly she sought refuge in a Pentecostal church, where she spent time fasting and praying for deliverance.

After a particularly violent incident with Hannah which led to Ada staying in hospital for two weeks, she at last began to question the wisdom of remaining in a marriage that was made in hell. She was compelled to recall her past, review her present and analyze her future. Looking at the situation strategically, she knew that a job for her husband would radically change the situation for good and reduce the tension in the family, but she felt that the current situation was unlikely to improve for the foreseeable future because there seemed to be no end in sight for the court case. Bello could not get another job at present because of negative references from his former employers, who seemed determined to strangle his chances of finding work. Also, he was financially incapable of starting his own business because of a lack of collateral and savings to secure a business loan. In any event, although he was a believer in capitalism, Bello lacked both knowledge and experience of how to create wealth through self-enterprise or creative capitalism. It was clear to Ada at this stage that her options were either to stay in the marriage or to abandon the sinking ship.

However, if she stayed in the marriage she feared that

the circle of violence, abuse, financial hardship and degrading treatment that she and her daughters had endured for the last three years might get worse. It would be only a matter of time before something terrible happened to her, which would in turn expose her daughters to even more abuse and violence at the hands of Hannah. By contrast, a divorce or separation might bring shame to her father and her family, but it would mean that she and her daughters would be removed from danger and constant exposure to abuse and violence. It would at least usher in the opportunity for them to enjoy some measure of peace and tranquillity, wherever they might go – and might even offer Ada the golden chance to begin a new life and realize her ambitions at last.

Ada concluded that she had made enough sacrifice for her husband and her father's family, and that the time had come for her to make sacrifices instead for herself and her daughters. Accordingly, she decided on separation and planned her escape to the city with military precision. On the fateful day of her departure, she gathered up all her jewellery, savings and other easily convertible valuables. With tears rolling down her face, she glanced for the last time at the family home – a place that had provided her with immense joy and happiness before her world had collapsed during the last three impossible years.

And so Ada and her daughters left for the city, without giving any notice to her husband, her parents or her neighbours. She hoped that she would return some day as a happy and fulfilled woman.

7

Life in the City

Ada and her children arrived in the city without the vast
majority of their possessions, due to the extreme
circumstances that had surrounded their escape from the
family home. A family friend provided them with
accommodation for the first two months, before Ada
secured a two-room apartment on a one-year lease agreement in a run-down area of the city. The neighbourhood
was light years away from the kind of lifestyle and comfort
zone they were used to. The accommodation Ada rented
formed part of a massive house that had seventeen other
separate rooms and was fully occupied by other families.
It was the cheapest accommodation that she could find,
and the only kind she could afford, considering her other
liabilities. The area was filthy and noisy without essential
amenities or an accessible road. Ada soon realized that the
electricity supply in the city was not only spasmodic, it
also depended on your class, where you lived and,
crucially, how the provider felt on the day. These factors
determined whether you would get any supply and for how
long. Generators had become the order of the day for those
who could afford them and were prepared to put up with
the noise. Gas was also something of a luxury, expensive

and regularly in short supply. The poor who lived in such run-down neighbourhoods as Ada's had to improvise, depending on their respective needs. Ada was also shocked to discover that water supply was a big problem. She and her daughters had to walk a few streets away to buy water for drinking and washing. Such was their baptism into the reality of life in the city. Previously, of course, they had enjoyed all these amenities without difficulty.

More worrisome for Ada was the general environment, which was not suitable for bringing up children who were used to better things in life. Just like every run-down neighbourhood in every overcrowded inner city, the population was infested with shoddy characters and a criminal underworld. Ada feared that her daughters' impeccable characters and exemplary manners might be compromised and heavily influenced by the unruly characters in the neighbourhood if they stayed in the area for too long. Furthermore, general hygiene generated her worst fears, as the house had only four poorly maintained toilets and three bathrooms without a single kitchen. Her only consolation was that her children were quick and happy to adjust to their new environment, which they said was far better than the exposure to unending abuse, violence and humiliation they had been subjected to previously.

With the accommodation problem out of the way, at least for the time being, Ada turned her attention to securing school admission for her daughters and to seeking employment for herself, or an opportunity to engage in some kind of wealth-creating enterprise with her remaining savings. Ada soon realized that these tasks and challenges would test her resolve, wit, determination and endurance to their limits. With four girls to feed, clothe and pay school fees for, she knew that it was going to require a herculean effort, and much luck, but she was determined to survive. She sold some of her jewellery to raise school fees and pay for their accommodation for the first year. Admission was secured in a school far removed from what the girls were accustomed to, but again, her daughters surprised her with their flexible approach to life. Ada also quickly found a clerical job in a small family company, but she resigned after just three months because it was not challenging for her and the pay was so infinitesimal, it did not even make a dent on their expenses. However, she soon identified a gap in the market for fruits and vegetables in her neighbourhood. After some thorough market research, she established a thriving business and within a very short period she was recording three times her previous monthly pay in just one week.

For over two years, Ada and her daughters remained happy and united as they settled well in the city. The girls adjusted to their new school environment with remarkable ease. Ada's business was flourishing and it provided enough money for essentials like school fees, rent and food, with a little extra for savings. Ada was no longer living in fear of the violence and humiliation that had previously plagued her life. Her attention was focused on her business and she was looking forward to expanding when another unexpected disaster struck. Without notice, the local authority decided to demolish all illegal structures by the roadsides, and this included the stall Ada rented from her landlord near a notoriously busy junction, which had proved to be such a good location for her business. This was a major disruption and disappointment for Ada, as she was suddenly left with no alternative place for her business except a dedicated fruit market situated in another part of the city. At that time of year, she knew she would have a problem securing a free stall at the market, let alone affording the rent for it.

The situation progressed from bad to worse as the month went by without any income to pay another round of school fees which would be due a few months later. However, Ada hoped that things would improve and that she would find a business, pay the rent and use the balance to invest in the products without falling into the danger of having to use her capital to pay the school fees. In desperation to acquire another business unit, and forgetting that she lived and operated in an area dominated by criminal minds, Ada asked her customers to spread the word for her and to look out for suitable premises. Her innocent but mistaken action was a recipe for disaster and the beginning of her downfall. It was a classic case for heartless, merciless '419' criminal gangs, who immediately saw her as a potential *mugu* or *mumu* (victim or fool) and seized the opportunity to exploit her vulnerability for their own gain.

As Ada was to explain it later, 419 is the code under Nigerian criminal law which refers to some classified financial and economic activities. The offences are popularly referred to as '419', and the gangs who commit these crimes are the scumbags of society – the new breed of Nigerian criminals whose activities are now known all over the world. They have perfected their methods over time and, remarkably have successfully created a layer of economy-within-the-economy which seems to grow faster than the wider Nigerian economy. It was sad for Ada to concede, but these criminal gangs have engineered and developed sophisticated strategies, some of them so truly ingenious that it was almost impossible for her not to admire the amount of time, the quality of work and the brainpower involved. They included an elaborate web of lies, deceit and tricks designed to extract money from their victims. Even for the few victims who bother to conduct some degree of due diligence, the storylines, lies and various strategies they use are so overwhelmingly compelling and convincing that the victims are left without much room to extricate themselves, and once they are committed it is too late. The favourite weapon in the armoury of these gangs is without any doubt information technology. They use e-mail, Skype, fax, mobile phones and Facebook to identify targets, to send and receive information and to groom their victims.

The gangs and their associates are master forgers and identity fraudsters too with unimpeded access to sophisticated machines and equipment used to produce fraudulent but high-quality documents and other materials designed to persuade victims that the transactions and documentation are genuine. They assume fake identities and have developed affinities with other criminal gangs abroad who provide them with valuable information and the identities of their victims. They attach high value to anonymity in their operations, but in cases of large-scale operations involving mega-money and where the potential victim has insisted on visitation, the inspection of equipment or a factory, or a face-to-face meeting, the gangs go to great lengths to rent the desired factory, equipment or office (including government offices). Victims, however, are usually naive or greedy participants who consciously or unconsciously think that they can get something for nothing. They often conduct little or no due diligence, regardless of how incredible, dubious or bizarre the offer may be. The attraction of quick money and a quick fix often clouds their better judgement and easily betrays their desperation or vulnerability, which are then exploited so mercilessly by the 419 gangs.

In Ada's case, a well-dressed gentleman came to her home one evening and introduced himself as Mr Emmanuel. He claimed to have purchased some fruit and vegetables from her recently and said that he had found a suitable location for her business. Even though she did not recognize this fellow as one of her familiar customers, which ought to have set the alarm bells ringing, her interest was aroused. With a mixture of excitement and desperation, Ada asked to know more about the property and the rent. To whet her appetite and maintain her enthusiasm, Mr Emmanuel advised her that the better business approach would be for her to view the property first in order to assess its size, condition and location, and then she could decide whether or not it was appropriate for her type of business.

A date was agreed and a few days later, Ada went to view the empty shop. She fell in love with it instantly: size, condition, location and area were all perfect. It was near a big, busy junction of four major roads, in a middle-class area with well-maintained, large pedestrian spaces. More significantly, the area had good security and the shop was properly protected with lock-up facilities. Ada would simply leave her goods in the shop at the end of the day, eliminating the need to carry them back home as had been the case with her former shop. She was desperate to rent the premises and was determined to conclude matters as soon as possible, but she was told that the owner of the shop was busy in his office in another part of the city and would only be free in two days' time.

Ada met Mr Emmanuel again on the agreed day and they went to meet the landlord. He made it known to Ada that the shop had been attracting huge interest, but that most prospective tenants were not serious. He warned that he was not prepared to waste his time with Ada if she was not serious. Ada immediately confirmed her real desire to lease the shop and added that she had a sizeable deposit to make if they agreed on the rent price. Ada was happy with the rental value, but was worried by the landlord's insistence on a two-year tenancy instead of one year. She eventually agreed to rent the shop for the initial period of two years because she had done her calculations and came to the conclusion that she would have enough money left to fill up her shop and pay the final-year school fees for her eldest daughter Amina. She also knew that the two-year tenancy would grant her the freedom to focus her attention on how to make enough money to pay the next house rent and the school fees for her other daughters. Ada left a deposit and promised to come the following day to complete payment and sign the necessary lease documents.

When she returned to the landlord's office to complete the payment as agreed, she was amazed to see a lady and another gentleman who were apparently willing to pay a higher rent for a longer period. However, the landlord reassured her that if she agreed to extend the lease period by another year at the agreed rate, he would let the shop to her. Ada considered her options and came to the conclusion that she had already made a commitment and backing out now meant losing the shop and missing a great opportunity to start generating a quick income through her business. Conversely, she reminded herself that the need to make a greater commitment now meant that she would have to sacrifice either the money already earmarked for Amina's school fees, or the business itself. Either way she had clearly been pushed into a very tight corner and was now in a dilemma, having to make a difficult decision under intense pressure. In full knowledge that rival 'prospective tenants' were waiting in the wings to rent the shop at a higher price, she was forced to make the desperate decision to accept the increased offer. For the second time, she was unable to read the danger signs.

Ada was given an ultimatum to complete her payments by the end of business that day, otherwise she would miss the chance to rent the shop. She hurried home to get the money and returned to the office to complete the lease documents. She was told to be at the shop at 9 a.m. the following day, when the security staff would be there to unlock the premises. Although Ada knew that she had taken a lot of risks in the process of securing the shop, she was happy that it was over and that she now had premises for her business and could once again start generating some income, now a matter of urgency.

Ada went to the shop the following morning as instructed and waited until 9.45 a.m. When the security staff failed to show up, she called the landlord. This supposed landlord politely apologized and informed her that she had not yet paid the agency fee, which was 20% of the total value of the rent plus another 10% local authority land rate. Ada went berserk, venting her frustration at the landlord whom she accused of exploiting her and failing to mention these overheads earlier in the process. Those fees were normal practice in the industry, she was told – she was free to check that out with other people if she wished. She was further advised to return to the office the following day for a refund if she was not happy to pay the extra fees. Driven by her desperation to resume her business and considering her commitments thus far, Ada opted to extend her risk yet again and proceeded to the office to make the payment, depleting her business account still further in the process. She was directed once again to return to the shop by 9 a.m. the following morning to gain access to the premises. For the third time, Ada failed to read the danger signs.

Ada duly attended the shop the following morning, and this time the shop was open with about five people engaged in cleaning work. Ada walked into the shop feeling very happy that her landlord had not disappointed her this time. But her happiness soon turned to anger as she was told by one of the cleaners that the cleaning contract had been commissioned by another tenant who had recently rented the shop. This triggered further rage from Ada, who immediately tried to call both the landlord and Mr Emmanuel. She soon discovered that their respective phone lines were dead. After repeated attempts to contact them without success, she proceeded to the landlord's office. There she met workers moving furniture from a lorry into the office for, they said, the new tenants who were shortly moving in. They knew nothing of the previous 'tenant' with whom she had been dealing. Ada came to the shocking realization that she had fallen victim to a 419 criminal gang.

Ada was financially ruined and emotionally heartbroken, devastated to discover that the entire venture had been a massive scam – all of it, from Mr Emmanuel's first approach, through the story of the potential rival tenants, to the landlord's claim of extra agency fees. Ada had failed at every stage to identify the warning signs, because she had not asked the right questions or conducted any form of due diligence. She had simply and tragically been overpowered by the urge to acquire business premises quickly, because she had an acute need to generate income to meet her pressing liabilities.

She had no wish to attempt the recovery of her money. To start with, she felt shocked, devastated and mentally weak after what had happened. She felt unable to summon up the courage to initiate yet another long fight which would undoubtedly require enormous mental endurance. Also, she was realistic in her appreciation of the difficulties occasioned by her failure from the beginning to conduct due diligence on the backgrounds of these fraudsters, which ought to have unmasked their true identities, addresses and any possible risk points. Without proper details and evidence, she knew that it would be difficult, if not impossible, to trace and recover her money. The documents they had given her were most likely to be fake.

Furthermore, she was aware that in the police and legal systems bribery, corruption and inordinate delays were endemic and institutionalized. Equally, she was concerned that she lacked the financial muscle required to be able to pay her legal bills as well as grease the palms of police and judicial officers to encourage them to perform their respective duties. Perhaps more significantly, Ada was worried that she had no reliable and trusted contact within the police and legal systems to provide her with advice and guidance during the process, which most definitely would make her a sitting target for exploitation by other 419 criminal gangs within these systems. After careful thought, she decided that the risks associated with any attempt to recover her money from the criminal gangsters were greater than the benefits. Consequently, she decided instead to limit her losses and accept this bitter experience as a major setback and another layer of misfortune in a troubled young life. Ada hoped that this no-nonsense approach would help to relieve some of the pain and liberate her to focus her attention on the future.

She quickly reviewed her finances to enable her to adjust her plans, prioritize needs and develop appropriate survival strategies for both the short and long term. She soon realized the depth of her financial exposure and vulnerability, with both her business and savings accounts significantly depleted. She was left with only her jewellery and a limited amount of money to feed her family and to pay school fees for one of her four daughters. Her priority was Amina, her eldest daughter, who was in her final O Level year. Ada opted to settle Amina's school fees and, in the unlikely event that the situation remained the same, she planned to activate her reserve option of using her valuable jewellery as collateral to borrow money in order to finance her business and pay school fees for her other daughters if and when they became due.

Unfortunately for Ada, there were no positive changes in the family fortunes for many months. She settled Amina's school fees, ensuring that her daughter could complete this essential phase of her education. However, this was followed three months later by a demand notice from the school stating that the fees for her other daughters should now be paid. One week after the fees were due, her three younger daughters were sent back home by the school for their non-payment. This extreme action sent shockwaves through Ada and jolted her into taking desperate but ultimately unsuccessful measures.

Still in a panic, she left her children at home the next morning and went to her uncle to ask for a bridging loan. This ended in disappointment when he refused to help. Ada then met a friend later that day who introduced her to a dealer in second-hand jewellery. The jeweller noticed Ada's desperation and quoted a price far below the real value of her jewellery. She was disappointed to have to sell her precious possessions for less than they were worth, but this was a difficult time. She comforted herself with the thought that the sacrifice was necessary in order to secure her children's education, which she held to be the best investment any parent can make for a child. By the time Ada and the dealer had agreed on the price, however, it was too late to go to the bank. They arranged to meet at a nominated bank the following morning.

However, while Ada was away making frantic efforts to raise the money for her children's school fees, two separate events were taking place both within and outside her home. Each would have tragic consequences for the family. The first incident related to Amina, who confided in a friend called Elizabeth that her siblings had been expelled from school because her mother was in serious financial difficulties and had not paid their fees. Elizabeth offered to help and arranged to visit Amina's family home that evening for the first time.

The second incident concerned Tunde, a middle-aged professional man and neighbour who was generally liked and respected within the neighbourhood. He noticed that Halima, one of Ada's twin daughters, was still at home looking very unhappy when she ought to have been at school. His curiosity got the better of him, so he decided to investigate. Halima was by now in a state of distress and crying uncontrollably, so he invited her into his room in an effort to calm her down. Halima told him that she had been suspended from school because her mother had not paid the fees due to financial difficulties. Tunde placed his hand across her shoulders in sympathy and immediately offered to pay the fees in the event that her mother was not able to raise the money.

Happy and excited at this news, Halima's instant and innocent reaction was to hug Tunde in appreciation of his kindness. He then offered Halima what seemed to be a drink of orange juice, she accepted in clear breach of her mother's rule not to take any drinks or food from strangers. Although Halima drank only half the contents of the glass, it was enough to cause the desired effect for Tunde. The young girl suddenly felt very dizzy and fell asleep within a few moments.

Tunde feasted on her unconscious body, violating and repeatedly raping her. When Halima came round a couple of hours later and began to recall the sequence of events, she realized that her drink had been laced with a drug and that she had been raped. She was angry and devastated that her privacy had been abused and her innocence stolen away in the most cowardly manner by a neighbour who had gained her trust and confidence by deceit, but who was in truth a paedophile, a rapist and a dangerous sexual predator. Tunde gave her the school fees and threatened her with immediate death if she told her mother or anyone else about the rape and the source of the money. When he judged the time to be right and safe, he smuggled Halima out of his room.

Ada returned home after an exhausting day to find Halima feeling unwell and complaining of a headache. She gave her some paracetamol and told her to get some rest. Later that evening, she told her daughters that she would go to the bank in the morning to get some money out and then would proceed to the school to pay the school fees. Amina advised her mother to suspend her plans until the arrival of her friend, who might offer an alternative rescue plan that could help her save her jewellery in the long run.

Ada was obviously concerned that Amina might have come into contact with dubious characters in the neighbourhood, which was known to be a breeding ground for men of the underworld. Who was this 'friend'? She was about to ask Amina the identity of the man she was expecting when Elizabeth was led to their rooms by one of the neighbours. After some formal pleasantries, Elizabeth gave Ada a careful account of her background, her job, how she had met Amina by chance in the neighbourhood, and her intention to help the family. Ada was curious and asked her why a very successful woman like her was still single. Elizabeth simply regurgitated a familiar excuse she must have used a million times before. She told Ada that she had spent time building a successful career at the expense of early marriage, in the hope that her success would be a magnet for potential husbands but to her surprise she later found that she was mistaken. Men seemed intimidated and scared of her success, perhaps because they thought it would make her feel too independent, accomplished and powerful.

Ada then asked why she wanted to help the family, and at what price. Elizabeth told her that her interest in Amina stemmed from her remarkable similarity to her own younger sister, who had tragically passed away five years earlier because of pregnancy and illegal abortion. She claimed that Amina walked, smiled and generally behaved like her sister and that she had taken Amina to her heart like the sister she no longer had. Elizabeth also claimed that her generosity was limited to her friendship with Amina, and that she was minded to assist the family at a difficult time only because she had some disposable income. Ada was therefore reassured that the offer of help was voluntary and that any acceptance ought to be voluntary too, with no strings attached, no hidden agenda and no short- or long-term consequences for the family.

Elizabeth offered Ada a large sum of money for food and school fees. She also offered to assist Amina to secure a well-paid job after her final O Level exams. Ada and her family were joyous and most grateful to Elizabeth for her extremely generous offer. To cement mutual trust and confidence in the relationship, Elizabeth agreed that the family might visit her home on a convenient weekend.

As they said goodbye, Ada felt so relieved: God had intervened at the right time to grant her family unexpected favours through Elizabeth. The school fee nightmare had temporarily ended, at least until the next academic year. She would no longer be forced by circumstances to sell her jewellery at ridiculously low value. And Amina was in a harmless, friendly relationship with a successful lady who could offer her purpose and direction, nothing to do with those hopeless men in the neighbourhood.

While her siblings were jubilant at the prospect of

resuming school, Halima was thrown into deep confusion and emotional turmoil. She was already suffering from depression as a result of the rape, confused as to what do with the money Tunde had given her for the school fees, and uncertain whether to confide in her mother about the rape. She spent the night wrestling with self-pity and self-criticism. Why had help only become available to the family *after* she herself had been drugged and violated? She also struggled with guilt at having contravened her mother's specific advice not to accept drinks from strangers or to enter a neighbour's room unaccompanied. She felt that her breach of that advice had created the opportunity for the monster to attack her.

Apart from the death threat from Tunde, Halima was fearful of disclosing her ordeal to her mother because it would not only cause her to explode like a ballistic missile: she would charge straight in to confront Tunde, thereby exposing the entire incident to public view. Halima feared that she would most certainly end up being a victim twice, and be stigmatized for life if news of the rape spread to her neighbours, friends and school. She questioned whether she was strong enough to carry that baggage for the rest of her life.

Furthermore, with the 'nice guy' reputation Tunde enjoyed in the neighbourhood, Halima felt that she might face a backlash from people refusing to accept her version of events. Some would go as far as questioning her motives for venturing into his room in the first place. Society generally, and the police in particular, didn't usually take matters like this very seriously – and at the end of the day people would mostly think that she had brought it on herself. In any event, the man had money to bail himself out of trouble even if her mother went the police. She was worried that he might also callously use the money he gave her to blackmail her. After careful consideration of all her options and the likely consequences, Halima decided to return the money to Tunde, to live with her experience, to say nothing about the rape and let sleeping dogs lie.

Ada and her children went off to school the following morning and while the children went to their respective classes, Ada proceeded to the office to settle the fees. Weekly activities for the family proceeded as normal for about two weeks after that, while Ada vigorously attempted to resurrect her business or to secure a good job as an alternative.

Halima, however, began to feel very funny in the mornings, culminating in two vomiting accidents at school right in front of her friends. The second occasion prompted an older friend with experience of early pregnancy and abortion to suspect that Halima might be pregnant. Halima understandably but innocently denied that suspicion with a look of embarrassment because of her age and genuine naivety. She told her friends that the sickness must be due to food poisoning or some other stomach bug. Halima was then surprised to hear a confession from one of her friends that she had suffered a similar experience in the past, which she had promptly discussed with her boyfriend, and then, with the help of her mother, she had secretly aborted the pregnancy without the knowledge of her father or anyone else.

Halima was advised to share her experience with her boyfriend, or to confide in her mother, in order to get the abortion done if necessary and before it was too late. Halima was alarmed by this development as she had no boyfriend per se, and she naively felt that the unfortunate chance encounter with Tunde could not result in a pregnancy. Halima was, in any event, afraid to mention the subject to her mother, who was aware that at just over fourteen years old she had no concept of men – but, on the other hand, Ada did not know about the rape incident either. Discussing the pregnancy with her mother would only add fuel to the fire and further escalate a complicated matter, because she would naturally demand to see the person responsible for Halima's condition. Halima was determined to stay in charge of the matter herself.

She secretly arranged a hasty meeting with Tunde, during which she described her experiences and the ominous observations of her friends. Tunde knew that if this became public he would be run out of the neighbourhood, in addition to risking the full force of the law for the act of raping and impregnating a fourteen-year-old girl, which would be elevated to murder if Halima died as a result of an illegal abortion. Any reaction to the uncomfortable news had to be quick, sensible and perfectly arranged. Any wrong move would be disastrous for him. He hurriedly booked an appointment with his doctor for the next day, with a view to conducting a pregnancy test on Halima. Tunde picked up Halima on her way to school the next morning and headed to the clinic, where doctors confirmed that Halima was certainly pregnant. Suddenly panicked, Tunde instructed the doctors to terminate the pregnancy forthwith. After a prolonged procedure, Halima returned home, feeling nagging pains.

Over the next three days, these pains worsened, but Halima summoned the courage to put on a brave face and continued to attend school as if nothing had happened. But at about midnight on the third day, Halima started to bleed profusely and was heard screaming at the top of her voice and complaining of unbearable stomach pains. With no ambulance service or car in sight to assist, Halima was carried in someone's arms to the roadside, where Ada managed to flag down a taxi that conveyed Halima to a nearby clinic. Sadly the clinic lacked basic equipment and there were no specialist doctors on duty. More importantly, there was no blood in the blood bank to effect a blood transfusion. Halima progressively weakened through excessive blood loss. Before she passed away, however, she managed to tell her mother about the circumstances of the rape by their neighbour Tunde, and his arrangement for her to have an abortion.

For Ada, the death of Halima was another tragedy in a life already dominated by a series of disasters and disappointments. The death of her daughter was particularly hard to bear because of the circumstances that had led up to it. Ada strongly believed that Halima's death had been preventable. She would still have been alive, but for two deadly yet avoidable factors that had conspired to have a catastrophic effect on her young life. The first was the loss of her father Bello's job, which had given rise to the inhospitable conditions at their home, triggering Ada's decision to flee with her daughters to the city for their personal safety. The second was the sudden collapse of her business and the bitter experience with fraudsters, which had contributed to her inability to afford the school fees, leaving Halima vulnerable to a rapist at home at a time when she was supposed to be at school. The rape and the subsequent illegal abortion that had claimed her life would not have occurred if Ada's business had been operational as before and yielding a good income. Equally, she would have had enough money to take Halima to a better hospital for more effective medical treatment. Ultimately, Ada laid the blame squarely on what she called her 'life companion and tormentor' namely poverty.

Before Halima's body was taken home for burial, Ada reported the circumstances of her daughter's death to the police. This resulted in the arrest of Tunde on suspicion of rape and murder. In addition to grieving for her daughter's death, Ada was also subjected to another round of pain and public humiliation: she was summoned before a council of elders by her husband Bello, who alleged that she had run off to the city with his children without his consent and that her reckless action had occasioned the death of Halima. The elders ruled against Ada and she was made to pay a large fine. Eventually, Halima was laid to rest in the family cemetery.

Ada returned to the city a few days after the burial and proceeded to obtain a progress report on the case from the police and the director for public prosecutions. She was told that the investigations were still ongoing and that Tunde had been released on bail. Ada felt hopeless and helpless in her efforts to get justice for her daughter without sufficient funds to grease the palms of public officials in a country notorious for endemic corruption across the entire system. Corrupt practices, scandalous delays and excessive bureaucracy were institutionalized. The police in particular were deficient in many areas of their operations, lacking proper equipment and skills in key areas such as forensic investigation.

More significantly, Ada was told by the officer in charge of the case that proving the charges against Tunde would be an uphill task because of 'monumental evidential challenges'. Halima had left little evidence, beyond her account that she was raped by Tunde who gave her money for school fees and later took her to the clinic where she had the abortion. She had not made a formal statement or provided the name and location of the clinic. If Tunde denied the allegations, as expected, the entire case would hinge on a great deal of expert forensic evidence that was well beyond current police capabilities to provide. Ada reluctantly left the matter in their hands and concentrated instead on providing for her remaining children. There was nothing else she could do.

Life at home basically went into slow motion for Ada and her children as soon as Halima was laid to rest. Although Ada tried her best to mask her own pain, she was faced with the daunting task of encouraging the children to move on with life – which felt like an almost impossible mission. Halima had been the comedian in the family, illuminating their home with rib-cracking jokes and humour. Her siblings could not believe that she had suddenly gone, never to come back. They had no chance to say goodbye. For Ayesha, Halima's twin sister, the situation was more acute: she completely shut down and became a virtual recluse. She disregarded every effort to persuade her to engage with others, eat food and go back to school. Until Elizabeth intervened, she also refused to adjust to living a life without her twin sister, who had shared every life experience with her up to that point.

The intervention of Elizabeth was looked on as a game-changer for the family, because it provided a new and positive perspective to their outlook. Elizabeth knew that the family was passing through a very difficult period which rendered them vulnerable and helpless. She seized the opportunity to consolidate her assimilation into the family with relative ease through regular visits and by being generous with cash and other gifts.

As part of her plot to solidify her position in their hearts, she elevated herself to self-appointed counsellor, advisor and motivator to the family. She used her motivational speeches to stimulate positive thinking and to stop the family accepting themselves as 'poverty property'. On one occasion she urged the family to regard the circumstances of Halima's death as a wake-up call and an opportunity to prevent similar misfortune befalling them in future by channelling all their energy into creating enough wealth to insulate them from the constant threat of poverty and its associated dangers. She argued that this would help divorce the family from poverty and the causes of poverty. This speech was so emotionally and passionately charged that it moved Ayesha to announce at the end that Elizabeth's words had brought renewed hope, drive, confidence and determination to the family. They accepted an offer to go on a weekend retreat at Elizabeth's home.

8

Elizabeth

One Friday evening, Ada and her family left as planned for their weekend at Elizabeth's home. The journey from their own neighbourhood to a more affluent part of the city lasted forty-five minutes, but it was a taste of the kind of hospitality that awaited them. Elizabeth had dispatched two chauffeur-driven luxury SUVs to ferry them across town. Although Ada and her family were fully aware that Elizabeth was a natural beauty and they suspected she was fairly rich, they had not contemplated the degree of ostentatious wealth that greeted them on arrival at her home.

They were personally received by Elizabeth, who gave them a guided tour of 'The House of Grace' and its surroundings. Ada soon came to the realization that Elizabeth possessed all the necessary ingredients to complement her ebony beauty and to make her a successful, rich woman – she had glamour, elegance, intelligence, ambition, a strong personality, a silver tongue, and a burning desire to succeed where lesser minds might fail. Although Elizabeth presented herself as an oil company executive, Ada discovered that she had many interests and was highly mobile, hopping between local

and international cities and rarely spending two consecutive nights in her own home.

Her house oozed luxury. On the way across town, the
driver had told Ada that Elizabeth was well known for her
addiction to fashion. Ada was overwhelmed when she
walked into Elizabeth's massive dressing room, which
looked like a high-end fashion boutique for the mega-rich.
There was a whole display of exclusive, expensive
handbags, shoes, clothes and perfumes bearing the best
designer names from the fashion world. The wristwatch
section contained timepieces by Rolex, Breitling,
Blancpain and Cartier.

Elizabeth's other addiction was clearly information
technology and telecommunication gadgets – the house
was littered with different laptops, iPads, iPods and other
smart phones, with all kinds of Blackberry topping the bill.
Ada was amazed to observe that her handbag was rather
like a cab office, with several phones ringing simul-
taneously almost every minute. Elizabeth seemed adept at
juggling the different calls. She claimed to habitually carry
four different types of phone at any given time because of
network problems across the country. Ada was later told
that Elizabeth actually had different phones for different
'classes' of people, one of which was her family. This
helped her to discriminate between calls more effectively.
And depending on the occasion and her outfit, she
swapped SIM cards into her next choice of phone at will.

The House of Grace was a luxury five-bedroom home
with two separate three-bedroom flats at the back, located
in a leafy area of the city and furnished like a royal palace.
The main house had a twenty-five seater cinema hall, two
large sitting rooms, a dining hall and an out-of-this-world

kitchen that was enough to make any woman of taste jealous. All the bedrooms in both the main house and the flats were self-contained with ensuite bathrooms. The compound was filled with the latest luxury cars – Mercedes-Benz, BMW, Audi, Porsche, Toyota and Lexus. Not surprisingly, the floors were immaculate, and in the garden the grass and flowers looked very well manicured. Elizabeth had a security man, a housemaid who looked after her wardrobe and the spotless interior of the house, a cook, and a gardener who was responsible for the exterior of the house. Ada saw enough to conclude that whatever Elizabeth claimed she was doing, she was certainly good at it.

Ada and her children returned to the main house after the guided tour for dinner and entertainment. They were spoilt for choice: the menu was packed with local, oriental and continental dishes, all of them delicious. After dinner the family were escorted to their respective bedrooms to rest in splendour. Sleeping in different rooms was a remarkable change, and certainly a great pleasure for the family who had crammed themselves into two rooms ever since they had arrived in the city. The girls had time to shower and refresh themselves, but the urge to reassemble in their mother's room for a few minutes' gossip was simply irresistible. So they gathered to marvel at this extraordinary environment and to discuss what they had seen since their arrival at Elizabeth's home.

Amina in particular felt so intoxicated by it all, she was motivated to declared war immediately against poverty and the causes of poverty. Her strong view was that poverty had held the entire family in bondage for too long. As a result the family had suffered nothing but death, pain, humiliation and paralysis in their individual and collective quest for development. She promised them all that she would do her utmost to liberate the family from the clutches of poverty and bring them riches and comforts.

Ada herself confessed to feeling fear, intimidation and embarrassment at her surroundings and at the scale of wealth on display. She wondered how Elizabeth, thirty years old and still single, had managed to accumulate such wealth legally and unaided by any man or her parents. Ayesha conceded that it would be impossible for them to return happily to their own neighbourhood after being exposed to such luxury. She suggested that her mother should explore the possibility of Elizabeth allowing them to occupy one of her guest flats temporarily until things improved for them. But Ada wisely advised that it was imperative for the family to maintain their dignity, regardless of their present situation. They did not, she said, want to open themselves up to abuse, ridicule or exploitation. On that note she sent her daughters to their rooms to grab some much needed sleep in readiness for the busy day ahead.

Elizabeth seemed determined to offer her guests an unforgettable weekend. She packed the Saturday with activities that included a trip into town for sightseeing, shopping, lunch and the cinema. She splashed out on gifts, presents and foodstuffs for the family to take back to their home. The biggest surprise came when Elizabeth announced that she had organized a party in their honour that evening. The party went on into the night and was well attended by Elizabeth's high-society friends, wealthy neighbours and their children. Amina at her most elegant was the star attraction of the evening – and it was a good thing that Elizabeth was on hand and in control, shielding her from the admiring and greedy eyes of some of the men. Ada and her family mixed well with the party crowd and generally had a wonderful night.

All the guests who stayed over in the flats woke up very late on the Sunday and were treated to a light breakfast in bed. Some hours later, all the guests congregated in the dining room of the main house for lunch. After lunch, Elizabeth retired with Ada and her daughters to share some private moments, and as they packed up she presented them with yet more gifts and money. Ada and the girls did their best to express their appreciation for Elizabeth's generosity and hospitality in granting them the opportunity to share her wonderful home for the weekend. At last Ada and her reluctant daughters departed in style back to their own neighbourhood, with Elizabeth personally leading the convoy.

Although the family was sad to return home, they all agreed that the weekend getaway had been a good idea: for a while they had left behind all their problems, which had temporarily evaporated thanks to the distraction of Elizabeth's beautiful home and the busy round of activities she had organized. Ayesha further confessed that the experience had made her feel as if she had been born again, totally revitalized. She believed that she now had a compelling reason to live, namely to avenge her twin sister's death by rejecting poverty and engaging positively in wealth creation to avoid a repetition of what had happened to her dear sister.

For her part, Ada was thankful for the sudden help from Elizabeth, but deep down she was feeling concerned and suspicious about the source of her wealth as well as the motives for her sudden generosity, hospitality and kindness. Was this simply the action of an innocent Good Samaritan, or was Elizabeth some kind of manipulative monster with sinister motives designed to plunge Ada's family into yet more disaster? On second thoughts, however, Ada decided that her bitter experiences might have influenced her to be unfairly suspicious of Elizabeth's motives. She persuaded herself to grant Elizabeth the benefit of the doubt.

Unfortunately, and unbeknown to Ada at that time, her first suspicions were not far from the truth. Elizabeth may have been beautiful, and generous with her wealth, but underneath she was a woman with a very dark side. As Ada and her family would later find out, Elizabeth was ruthless, single-minded, highly manipulative, exceptionally greedy and a hardened risk-taker. To Elizabeth, there was no freebie or free lunch. Her motto was 'Use what you have to get what you need'. And she believed in getting what she wanted by any means necessary and regardless of the obstacles.

Right from her first encounter with Amina during an unconnected visit in her neighbourhood, when she spotted the girl looking extraordinarily beautiful in her school uniform, Elizabeth knew that she had discovered a money-making machine. She proceeded to stalk Amina, spending time waiting for her outside her school. For Elizabeth, Amina was a valuable raw gem: with some delicate grooming, she hoped to transform the girl into a formidable winning asset. Amina already possessed youth, beauty and a shapely body. Her neighbourhood strongly suggested to Elizabeth that Amina's parents must be very poor, which would probably make the girl vulnerable, desperate and hungry for money and the luxuries money could buy. Elizabeth concluded that closer contact and observation over time would help reveal whether or not Amina possessed other crucial qualities not readily seen from a distance.

After the first contact with Amina, the next challenge for Elizabeth was the tricky and gradual process of winning her trust, confidence and loyalty. As a seasoned professional, she quickly devised a plan to pick Amina up secretly in one of her luxury cars at agreed times within the neighbourhood or at the school gate, taking her to various top food and fashion shops and buying expensive gifts for her. At this stage, Ada knew nothing about Elizabeth and was not aware of her existence. Amina did not realize it, but the gifts, food, quality time and general exhibition of wealth were not mere freebies and expressions of love for a young friend: they were part of a calculated scheme of recoverable investments. During this 'observation period', Elizabeth concluded that Amina possessed the vital qualities she was looking for: intelligence, confidence, fearlessness, tenacity and a burning desire to succeed. Perhaps more significantly for Elizabeth's purposes, Amina was also very naive and vulnerable and had shown a huge hunger for money. She was therefore now certain that it would be easy to 'remote-control' Amina's life for her own gain.

Amina loved every moment of that good time. The attraction seemed mutual, though it was obvious to Amina from the out set that they came from different worlds. Elizabeth seemed to her to hail from some extraterrestrial world with the power to acquire outrageous wealth, while she herself came from a world plagued by misfortune and abject poverty. Amina was fascinated and thrilled by Elizabeth's beauty, personality, appearance, class and taste. It was an irresistible temptation to adopt Elizabeth as her role model and mentor. She had now seen enough wealth and luxury to tickle her hunger and determination to engage in wealth creation. She wanted nothing further to do with poverty. With firm assurances from Elizabeth of help following her O Level exams, Amina made a personal vow to do whatever it would take to be and live like her role model, and to extricate her family from the grip of poverty. For some time, in accordance with instructions from Elizabeth, she successfully managed to keep her friendship secret from her mother until the whole school fee saga blew up, ending in Halima's death and the formal introduction of Elizabeth to the rest of the family.

By the time Ada and her family left Elizabeth's house after their weekend stay, Elizabeth was ecstatic: her mission to secure the trust of the whole family had been successful. She knew that Amina would soon complete her basic education and would then, as agreed, turn to Elizabeth for help in finding well-paid employment. The time was now right to put into action stage two of her plan, which was to begin the gradual process of grooming Amina. The aim of this stage was to prepare Amina adequately to play her intended role with distinction and to gain absolute control and domination of her, ensuring unequivocal loyalty and easy manipulation of every aspect of her life. The plot involved beginning a lesbian relationship with Amina, and during this period brainwashing her to develop a real hatred for men. Elizabeth wanted to achieve the total extermination of any emotional feelings Amina might have for men, which would be crucial for her future role. To this end, she concocted a convincing storyline to persuade Amina to spend another weekend at her home, this time without the company of her sisters or mother.

Elizabeth made an impromptu visit to Ada two weeks after the family's weekend retreat, when she informed Ada that her good friend who was the CEO of a sister company would be coming to town for a conference and that she would be staying in Elizabeth's house rather than at a hotel. She persuaded Ada to allow Amina to spend the weekend at her home so that she could facilitate an informal, one-to-one meeting between her friend and Amina to discuss job opportunities.

A driver was duly sent to pick up Amina on Friday evening. Once at Elizabeth's house, she was introduced to the friend, Matilda. However, soon after the introduction Matilda excused herself and retired to her room for a rest, saying she was exhausted by her long journey. Amina relaxed for while before she was led to Elizabeth's own bedroom, where she was surprisingly told she should feel free to sleep on the bed whenever she was ready. Elizabeth joined her half an hour later, carrying flowers and expensive gifts which Amina naively accepted with thanks and without reading any meaning into the gesture.

With the lights turned out, they settled themselves to sleep. A short while later, however, Amina was woken by a hand running uncomfortably along her body. At first she thought that it was a mistake, but she soon realized it was a deliberate act as the hand kept coming back each time she removed it from her body. Elizabeth spent a large part of the night preaching about her deep love and affection for Amina and promising to take good care of her. Shocked and embarrassed that a responsible lady she so much respected was talking to her about a woman-to-woman relationship – an idea which was alien to her – Amina protested her innocence and resisted the pressure from Elizabeth. Clearly in distress and shaking, she sought refuge in her age, pleading that she was still a virgin and was ignorant of what Elizabeth was requesting of her. She also argued that what Elizabeth was requesting of her was in fact forbidden by her religion as morally reprehensible behaviour. Her pleas fell on deaf ears.

Amina's refusal suddenly ignited rage in Elizabeth, who began to exhibit the aggressive and threatening tendencies she had so far kept well hidden. She threatened to throw Amina out of the house, warned her that she would withdraw her promise to help Amina find employment, and accused Amina and her family of being ungrateful after all that she had done to help them. She then reminded Amina that men had brought nothing but pain, death, misery, poverty and calamity to her family, and that Elizabeth was the only person who had shown compassion, love and care for them.

Elizabeth went on to wage further emotional war by reminding her about what Tunde had done to Halima, what her grandfather had done to Ada, how her own father had treated them all before they ran away to the city, and how Ada had been duped by men which had led to the collapse of her business. This emotional and psychological torture triggered a flood of bad memories that become too much for the young, innocent and vulnerable Amina to bear. This, together with the fear that Elizabeth would withdraw her help for the family, left Amina believing she had no option but to give in. The adverse consequences for the family were too much to contemplate if she continued to refuse. Eventually she caved in: 'Auntie Lizzy,' she said, weeping, 'you are taking advantage of my family's vulnerability to abuse me. But go ahead and violate me. I have no other choice.'

Elizabeth heartlessly proceeded to rape Amina, deaf to her emotional pleas. Both during and after the ordeal, Amina felt shocked, frozen, disgusted, violated and humiliated. She cried throughout.

Having satisfied herself, and feeling on top of the world after the horrible ordeal she had forced Amina to go through, Elizabeth spent the rest of the night and the following morning endlessly preaching her love for Amina and reassuring her that she and her family would no longer lack anything. Amina duly had the scheduled one-to-one meeting with Elizabeth's friend Matilda, when some fanciful 'job experience' was provisionally offered. Still feeling utterly distressed, Amina was sent home with expensive gifts and cash as 'compensation' for her ordeal.

This cycle of expensive gifts, cash and sex repeated itself several times over many months until Amina had completed her time at school. During this period, Amina was brainwashed to believe that she must learn to use what she had to get whatever she needed; that only Elizabeth would provide her with love, care and protection; that genuine love could only come from a lesbian relationship; that Elizabeth would help her to acquire the riches she wanted; and that she must not open her heart to any man because they would break her heart, cheat on her and ruin her life. Just as Elizabeth planned, Amina lost interest in men over time.

With the lesbian relationship in full swing, Elizabeth

spent quality time, effort and money on grooming and instilling in Amina some of the essential skills and habits that were required for the role she wanted Amina to play – without, of course, revealing her motives. Amina finally finished her exams and Elizabeth decided that the time had come not only for Amina to start to create and accumulate wealth, but also for Elizabeth to reveal to her how she was going to become a money-making machine for both of them. Elizabeth duly told Ada and Anima that her friend Matilda, the CEO of an oil company, wished to employ Amina as a trainee personal assistant, which would require Amina to commute frequently and at a moment's notice. She suggested that Amina should attend a formal interview. They all agreed that Amina would spend the weekend with Elizabeth so they could fly out on the Monday morning to the corporate headquarters of the company in another city.

Amina arrived at Elizabeth's home on the Friday evening and after dinner they retired to the study for a discussion. Elizabeth now wanted to formalize an agreement on the rules of engagement that would govern their working relationship. First she demanded to know whether Amina was ready to divorce poverty and embark on the journey to wealth creation, whether she had the capacity to keep secrets, and whether she could be trusted. With massive excitement and eagerness written all over her face, Amina responded to all the questions with a resounding 'Yes!'

Fully aware of Amina's naivety, desperation and vulnerability, Elizabeth felt that extracting oral assurances alone might not be sufficient to protect her own interests and solidify her total control over Amina. So she went further and engaged a *dibia* to perform a 'blood oath ritual'. The ritual involved the *dibia* taking blood from both Elizabeth and Amina and mixing it with another secret liquid, known only to the *dibia*. They swore to trust and confide in one another, to protect, promote and defend their mutual interests, to commit undivided loyalty to the cause, not to betray or cheat each other, and not to reveal secrets to any third party.

The idea behind this oath was to instil a kind of perpetual fear in Amina and achieve absolute control, authority and domination over her. It was also designed to establish an artificial barrier by creating a superior relationship between Elizabeth and Amina, over and above the relationship between Amina and her family. With full confidence and trust that Amina would never betray her or reveal her trade secrets, Elizabeth now told Amina openly and frankly about the true nature of her business operations: she was involved in 'runs', 'parol' and other dangerous activities that earned mouth-wateringly high rewards. Amina, she said, would be concentrating on runs to gain experience first, before taking on more risks as she matured.

Elizabeth explained that 'runs' was a modified, modernized name for the oldest profession in the world – prostitution. The younger practitioners preferred the more up-to-date, glamorous name of 'corporate runs'. Parol, she said, was the act of grooming and organizing beautiful young girls for men in return for a percentage of their earnings, called 'commission'. Elizabeth added that in both cases it did not involve standing on street corners or going to nightclubs to seek customers. Rather, it involved meeting clients in hotel rooms and guesthouses in cities around the country, strictly on an appointment basis.

Elizabeth had two operations in action, she told Amina, each managed with deadly efficiency. She planned and organized her runs in the usual manner by receiving calls from clients and responding to them. The other operation was much larger and required a lot of management skills. She had a hardcore of fifteen beautiful young girls, carefully selected, groomed and trained, who worked for themselves and were well established in the industry, but Elizabeth was paid a percentage of their earnings if she recommended them to any of the fifty clients on her runs and parol contact lists. She also made money from them if she took them to parties, where they were given 'thanks-for-coming' envelopes. She told Amina that she would be part of this category of self-employed young girls. Elizabeth promised to arrange parols and parties for her until she had established herself.

Elizabeth further revealed that the industry was huge, segmented, highly competitive and hugely profitable. She warned Amina that it was equally very risky, and there were diseases and dodgy characters at every level on both sides – both service providers and clients alike. More frightening was the revelation that girls sometimes suffered beatings, gang rapes, non-payment of charges and even death, with body parts taken for ritual purposes. There were, she said, no set fees or charges because of the many variables involved. Elizabeth herself, however, claimed to specialize and operate at the very top end of the market, where the earning potential was simply mind-boggling. Her clients included top politicians, bankers, lawyers, oil company executives, foreign diplomats, foreign oil company personnel, celebrities, professional footballers, businessmen, top military personnel, high-profile public figures and drug barons with lots of money to waste. Generally her fees were agreed in advance, unless the client was a familiar one and generous. Payments were generally made by bank transfer.

Contacts were usually made through recommendations by friends (parol) or by building an independent contact list as a girl progressed in the business. Having a list of contacts and building up experience helped to filter the good clients from the bad guys and the generous clients from the stingy ones. Elizabeth kept her various client lists stored on different phones, which helped her to decide when to take or reject business calls. For example, she told Amina she had a list containing twenty mega-rich clients that she must respond to immediately when their calls came through, and another list of rich clients she might go to or might send her protégés on parol.

The services offered were mostly of a sexual nature, she explained, but being ingenious, she had also diversified into other lucrative but dangerous areas – such as the murky world of intelligence-gathering, spying, snooping and extracting information from one client for another client, at a huge price. Clients in this category included rival politicians, wives, husbands, people in serious relationships and corporate clients.

Elizabeth further revealed that her clients liked exceptionally beautiful young girls with smooth skin, fantastic figures, no fat or stretch marks. Personal hygiene and regular testing were a top priority, a must for all her girls, in order to protect them and her clients, the majority of whom were popular faces and in serious relationships. Tools of the trade included condoms, two bank accounts, the latest fashion outfits and accessories, and at least two smartphones, preferably Blackberry. The girls used the phones to share erotic personal photos amongst themselves, which helped to secure referrals that earned them a percentage of the agreed fees. So if a client needed the services of another girl, the photo gallery could be activated for the client to make his choice, and once the fees had been agreed, the other girl would be notified and given the details of her appointment with that client.

Elizabeth also made huge sums of money from contracts awarded by her clients to supply beautiful young girls at private functions such as birthday parties, private dinners, government functions and end-of-year company parties. It was customary for the host to give each girl an envelope stuffed with cash as a thank-you for attending. Some of the girls might end up spending the night with clients, while others might just exchange contact details.

In addition to her general operating rules, Elizabeth taught Amina the other secrets of her success – the 'principles' which she said had kept her away from trouble and danger and had helped her to build and maintain her clients' trust and loyalty over the twelve years she had been in the business. There were five principles, she told Amina: keep clients' secrets confidential; never steal money or property from clients; only go with known or recommended clients; never follow a client to a private home; and treat each customer as a professional client to avoid emotional entanglements and rivalry

With all this experience behind her, she promised to mentor and train Amina all the way to the top – but only if Amina remained loyal to Elizabeth. Was Amina still willing to go down this road? Was she still committed to her ambition to become rich, to help her family sever all links with poverty? Amina replied emphatically, 'Yes! I want to start today!'

Wasting no time, Elizabeth made a phone call there and then to one of her mega-rich clients, known as 'Big Daddy'. She had secured a pretty, sweet young girl straight from school, she told him, a girl who had never been touched by a man. She teased Big Daddy with a description of Amina, and said that the girl was his if the price was right. Big Daddy promised to fly into town the very next day. A tough and experienced negotiator, Elizabeth persuaded Big Daddy that Amina was a special case and should therefore be exempted from the usual terms. They agreed on a separate, higher fee for a virgin. The sum they agreed on left Amina dumbfounded. It was an eye-opener. She had received her first lesson in negotiation skills and was excited by the amount of money that was out there to be made.

Next, Elizabeth and Amina concocted a story to feed Ada in the event of any delays that might cause Amina to return home later than the time agreed with her mother. Amina was delighted with the plans and looked forward to meeting Big Daddy. She couldn't wait for her first parol and her first big pay day. But in reality, Amina was boiling inside and waiting to erupt like a volcano. What she had been offered now by Elizabeth was a million miles away from what was previously promised. She was petrified about the prospect of starting a life as a professional prostitute at such a tender age. She had no concept of sex or men and therefore was understandably worried about some of the identifiable dangers and many of the unknowns in the trade. Her heart sank deep into her stomach from the beginning to the end of the lecture.

Amina began to contemplate how long she would be in the business, as well as the number, sizes and ages of men she would have to deal with during her time in the trade. She also worried about the dangers and risks that Elizabeth talked about such as death, injuries, diseases, violence, non-payment, gang rape, etc. She felt betrayed by how Elizabeth was able to combine deception, manipulation, lies and outright exploitation to gain her family's trust and confidence. Amina wondered how Elizabeth could have the temerity to proceed to exploit the state of her family's vulnerability to her own selfish advantage. She felt that Elizabeth lied about her background, lied about her sources of wealth, lied about getting her a good job and had now tricked her into becoming a professional prostitute.

She wondered what more harm Elizabeth was capable of inflicting on her and her family in future. Furthermore, Amina was troubled that she had taken a binding oath without any get-out clauses and was basically imprisoned in the relationship. This was particularly so as she did not know what the consequences would be if she opted out after discovering Elizabeth's secrets. Another source of worry for Amina was how she could look her mother and sisters in the eyes and maintain lies about her job in perpetuity.

Amina was so worried that she summoned the courage to ask Elizabeth why she embarked on all the lies and deceit and whether there was any alternative job to prostitution. But at the last minute she was frozen with fear of how Elizabeth would react and what the implications of her reaction would be. Amina pondered about the implications of not proceeding in accordance with Elizabeth's plans but she concluded that the risks were too high for her family.

Firstly, she did not know what the consequences of the oath would be for her and the family. Secondly, it had become obvious that Elizabeth was a nasty character and capable of killing her and harming her family, especially as she had discovered her secrets. Thirdly, what was on offer was realistically the only option available to help drag her family out of poverty and if she were to refuse the opportunity, her family would go back to square one – poverty. Amina concluded that she would rather do anything to stop her family sliding back into poverty. So, for the second time in her life, the fear of being left stranded in a vulnerable position with the threat of facing the unfortunate incidents associated with poverty, had forced her to try and make the best of the worst situation.

The reality of her situation persuaded Amina to think and act positively. Accordingly, she drew comfort and confidence from the fact that Elizabeth had been in the trade for at least twelve years, and with care and luck she had managed to create and amass immense wealth and was still in good health. Amina resolved that she would make the sacrifice in the manner proposed by Elizabeth for the sake of her family, with the self-promise to quit as soon as she had made enough money to establish them.

9

Amina's Secret Life

The next day, Elizabeth and Amina proceeded as planned to meet Big Daddy. To Amina's surprise, she was immediately swept off her feet. He was a very handsome man in his forties with expensive tastes in fashion and jewellery. His presence, authority and even his command of English seemed sensational to the teenager. Amina was amazed that a shy, innocent girl like herself who had no real concept of men before the meeting was already melting before he even touched her. Her actions instantly betrayed her, however, and Elizabeth, the seasoned pro, noticed what was happening and quickly took her to another room to calm her down and give her some stern advice.

Amina's encounter with Big Daddy went well under Elizabeth's supervision. He left the hotel early the next morning because of a busy schedule, but promised to return soon to spend some quality time with Amina. As it was her first time, Elizabeth insisted that Amina should spend the following day at the hotel as a precautionary measure so they could satisfy themselves that Amina had no injuries, pains or problems that might warrant a visit to the doctor. On her safe return home, Amina spent the next few days re-enacting her experience and imagining the colossal amount of money sitting in Elizabeth's bank account waiting to be transferred to her own.

She could not believe that the whole experience was so easy and that she could make so much money with so little effort. Elizabeth took Amina to her personal banker and with his help Amina opened a savings account, a business account and a current account. The proceeds from her encounter with Big Daddy were duly transferred. To avoid suspicion, Elizabeth advised Amina never to give away the extent of her new-found wealth to her family. Together they thought up a plausible story about her journey, her new job, and her plans to find decent accommodation for herself.

Amina returned home to meet her over-excited family, who were eager to hear all about her trip. Amina happily told her family that she had been offered the post of trainee personal assistant for a probationary period of one year, with the option of a permanent position after that if she did well. She added that the job would involve a lot of travelling with her boss, huge overtime payments and bonuses, a car and a housing loan. Her boss, she told them, had directed the accounts department to grant her application for a housing loan as a matter of urgency. They should be prepared to leave the neighbourhood very soon!

This news left the family in a frenzy, jubilant at the prospect of leaving that run-down neighbourhood for a better house with enough space for them all. Finally, good fortune seemed to be coming their way. Just one week later, the whole family moved to a comfortable house in an exclusive area of the city, well away from their former neighbourhood and a few miles closer to Elizabeth's house.

Over the next year, Amina made a great deal of progress in the business under the careful guidance and watchful eyes of her mentor. She had many referrals, and much help from Elizabeth who took her along to functions and private parties where she had opportunities to mingle with wealthy, high-profile clients. By the end of the year she had built up quite an impressive list of wealthy clients for herself.

Amina was so popular amongst her clients that she became inundated with requests for repeat business. Unless she was already engaged with another wealthy client, she never declined. She knew that the market was very fluid and that clients could always call the next favoured girl on their contact list if their first choice was not available. She was also aware that she would not make money if she was busy with another client when the next call came through. Repeated turning down of requests might drive away valuable clients in the long term. To mitigate her financial losses in that respect and also to maintain the faith of all her clients, she embarked on an aggressive recruitment programme to groom and train other young girls for referral (*parol*) purposes. She hoped that such measures would help earn her income when she was busy herself.

Recruitment was easy for her, because she still had many friends from school. She identified the most vulnerable ones from poor backgrounds who ticked all the boxes and were determined to work and earn good money to help insulate their lives from the poverty they were all too familiar with. Just as Elizabeth had done with her, she insisted on the secret oath-taking to ensure that she could maintain control, trust, confidence, loyalty and authority in relation to her recruits. Within a relatively short period of time, Amina metamorphosed from a shy schoolgirl into a streetwise operator. She felt she had come from gutter to glory almost overnight. She had come of age and learned the ropes, mastered all the tricks in the game, adopting and refining Elizabeth's rules of engagement along the way, and mastering the art of lying. It seemed that she could do no wrong as she managed her growing business empire meticulously, with military precision. By catapulting herself from rags to riches, Amina became the toast of her friends, who now aspired to be like her.

She adopted a zero-information policy in her efforts to protect her family and background, which she guarded jealously throughout this period. Her girls knew little or nothing about her. Her clients likewise had no knowledge of her background, and when she was asked about it, she simply reeled off her favourite claim that she had been raised in an orphanage. She had a dedicated phone line for her family and adopted the habit of never taking their calls in public.

Within a period of five years, Amina had amassed wealth beyond all her expectations. Prudently she entrusted the management of her wealth to her mother, in association with a pool of accountants, lawyers, estate agents, equipment managers and twenty-five other support staff. She had a fleet of expensive cars (mostly given to her on her birthdays), a portfolio of office blocks, expensive residential houses on leases, commercial warehouses, dredging machines and other earth-moving equipment all rented out on long leases to oil companies, and two four-star hotels. With plenty of money now available, she moved the family again to their own luxury pad in an affluent part of the city. Some of her siblings attended expensive private schools and went on to university. Even Ada went back to further education with a view to realizing her long-held ambition to become a lawyer.

Ada was very grateful and happy that Amina had redefined the family's existence and strategically repositioned it for the future by single-handedly removing the financial handicaps that had consistently plagued her family for years. But she nonetheless knew that the improved financial position would not bring final closure to all their troubles and worries. She felt a sense of emotional emptiness, imprisoned in bitterness and hatred because society forced her and her daughters to embark on a long treacherous walk on a lonely road littered with high hills and steep valleys simply on the basis of their gender.

The desire was to make them shrink as women but Ada survived this terrifying journey with her brain and mind defiantly intact and proceeded to record their present achievements. But her survival and accomplishments came with a price as they were exposed to too many dangers, obstacles and impediments and were subjected to all manners of inhumane treatment that gave rise to her bitterness and hatred. It also brewed and fermented poisonous emotional relationships between herself, her husband and his family as well as her own parents in those dark days before and during her arranged marriage. So, despite their remarkable survival and financial independence, complete happiness became a distant dream – illusive without the missing emotional link which troubled her for many years.

Ada held the view that it was imperative that the emotional emptiness had to be filled. She therefore believed that it was necessary to institute measures that would help to encourage a healthy relationship with her parents and husband on the one hand and her children with their father and grandparents on the other hand. So, riding on her reputation as a symbol of reconciliation, embodiment of forgiveness, a triumph for humanity and tranquillity personified, Ada planned to engage in the process of reunification, reconciliation, forgiveness and re-orientation with everyone in both her husband's and her father's families.

To achieve this task, Ada invested a lot of time providing Amina and her other daughters (who previously ruled out reconciliation) with a valuable education in dignity and forgiveness, encouraging them to set aside bitterness, vengeance and retribution in order to allow for tolerance, peaceful co-existence, collaboration and co-operation. Her daughters caved in after a prolonged resistance, to her greatest relief. With relationships restored to normal on all fronts, their achievements finally came to completion. Consequently, happiness and love returned to her two families and, with everyone working in harmony and unison to fight poverty, Amina proceeded to redistribute some of her acquired wealth to benefit both families.

First, Amina built two identical two-storey family homes in her father's town for her father and mother. She also provided huge financial support to her father and his second wife, Hannah, who had tormented them during those dark days. Amina equally provided money to her father to set up a successful business. Ironically, she secured a lifeline for her step-brothers' education by underwriting the costs of their tertiary education. During the reconciliation and reunification celebration in the family with everyone in attendance, her father and Hannah followed suit to render unreserved apologies to Ada and her children for the horrible treatment they individually and collectively were subjected to in the past. For Ada and her children, all the pain and suffering they passed through during those dark days instantaneously evaporated when they heard Bello and Hannah say, 'Ada, you and your daughters were the rejected stones a while ago but you have now become the cornerstones and the pillars that form the solid foundation of this house, may God bless you all.' Hannah asked for forgiveness for all her iniquities and behavioural deficiencies, which she blamed on immaturity, financial pressure and other determinants at the time.

Hannah's pleas were accordingly granted with some advice for the future. But going forward, Ada advised her to modify her approach to life and to always consider the likely consequences of her actions on other people, as those actions could have irreparable, devastating effects. She added that she and her daughters were only able to forget and forgive all that had happened in the past because they succeeded where other lesser minds would have been crushed under excruciating pain and suffering. She added that if the reverse were to be the case, they would have most certainly found it difficult to forget and forgive. Hannah was reminded that good could only come from this dark episode if Hannah would teach and instil in her children the need to always show understanding, consideration, conciliation, tolerance, kindness and general good towards other people they meet on their way to the top because they may meet the same people on their way down.

Secondly, Amina carried forward her agenda on

reconciliation, reunification and reorientation to her maternal home. She felt that it was right to extend her generosity and good fortune to her maternal home town as part of her endless determination to fight poverty. Amina was driven by her awareness that her mother's educational ambitions were ended prematurely, that her subsequent marriage was arranged and that her mother suffered tragic experiences, all of which created unpleasant tension that strained the relationship between her mother and her own parents over the years. Amina and her mother felt that a lot of water had now passed under the bridge since that period and that the time had come to look positively and progressively to the future.

Efforts were successfully made to normalise relationships and, thereafter, apologies were offered and accepted and everyone agreed to forgive and forget the past. Amina built an ultra-modern family home and bought an expensive car for her grandparents. She released her uncles from the burden of funding their children's education by granting the children comprehensive scholarships up to tertiary education level. As part of the reconciliation agreement, Amina also granted scholarships to many girls and women from primary to tertiary education levels in her grandfather's name, as a symbolic gesture and to further her grandfather's belief that women ought to have equal access to education amongst other things.

Furthermore, Amina and her mother embarked on a reorientation plan aimed at persuading her uncles/brothers to change their perception of women and their roles in the community and society as well as help to educate others. They argued that women possess immense talents that were underutilised in the communities and society because they have been stifled or suppressed by artificial barriers, discriminatory laws and behaviour, prejudices and negative attitudes, perceptions and stereotypes. Ada added that these artificial barriers deny women fair or equal access to education, job, business opportunities and other developmental opportunities that would have otherwise helped to empower and liberate women.

The empowerment, development, liberation and independence would have helped to generate the ambition and aspiration in women to aim high. Lack of empowerment and development of women meant that women's talents have not been cultivated and harvested, which also meant that a significant proportion of the population could not join a skilful national workforce or become entrepreneurs. Equally, the talents and value women bring to company boards, as well as national leadership and governance, would be denied or diminished. All this invariably would lead to low national productivity levels, low national growth and development and reduced national competitiveness in the global market. Importantly, these women would not be able to contribute meaningfully to the growth and development of their families and the communities they came from and married into.

To prove the inadequacies and deficiencies in the current system, as well as the old, irrational belief that women have no part to play once they marry out of their family home, community or wider society, they both cited themselves as case study examples. They argued that they had succeeded in helping to uplift their families (maternal and paternal) by their contributions thus far, which had helped to reduce poverty. They added that this only came about because of their respective empowerment, education and development, which turned them into successful and accomplished women.

Ada in particular cited her success in managing a huge Non-Governmental Organisation (NGO) in the city. She claimed to have flourished and recorded those successes because of her talents and access to education and opportunities that would otherwise have been denied or suppressed by artificial barriers. Ada strongly advised her brothers to ensure that their daughters were well educated as they were now all on scholarships. Finally, Ada ended the re-orientation exercise with her brothers and father by placing a poster on the wall and advising them to always bear the wording in mind each time they stepped out of the family compound. The writing on the poster says: 'Everyone is a winner but some of us are disguised as losers so don't let their appearance fool you.'

At this point, Amina could safely have claimed to have accomplished her primary goal of eradicating poverty from her family. There was ample evidence to suggest that she had brought the whole family successfully out of poverty, and – as things currently stood – had also insulated them from the danger of poverty in the future. They were now rich, and if they only looked after what they already had, they could remain comfortable and safe from poverty for the rest of their lives.

Amina could therefore have made a wise decision to retire with grace from the business of runs and parol. She did not do this. Greed, an over-riding desire to remain relevant in the game, and the lure of making tons of easy money overpowered her reasoning ability. She could not resist the temptation. The thrill, the buzz and the illusion of power were irresistible. Crucially, the illusory sense of immunity from the dangers associated with her trade impaired her ability to make the sensible decision to quit, even if she had wanted to. Regrettably, therefore, she carried on with her numerous clients and female lovers throughout this period. Her friendship and love for Elizabeth remained solid, but, apart from that very first encounter with Big Daddy, Amina was never emotionally involved with any man. She kept her services to her clients strictly professional, reserving her love only for their money.

The next three years witnessed dramatic changes in Amina's personal and business fortunes as she diversified and embarked on gigantic projects that required the injection of significant funds. Inevitably, she began to raise the risk levels in her personal and business ventures. On the personal side, she opted to provide her clients with services without protection, which attracted high rewards but was potentially dangerous to her health. On the business side she started to diversify into more dangerous business areas she really knew nothing about. Bit by bit, she was jettisoning her careful rules of engagement and going against the advice of her mentor Elizabeth.

One of the risky ventures she added to her portfolio was spying for her clients. She was effectively borrowing an idea from Elizabeth, who was a seasoned practitioner in the art of intelligence gathering. Elizabeth, however, was careful and skilful in performing this function for a handful of selected clients with whom she had built up a high level of trust, and she had no reported problems in over ten years of gathering intelligence for them. But Amina had no such experience before she started gathering intelligence for every Tom, Dick and Harry in a business that required practitioners to maintain absolute confidentiality, anonymity and secrecy. Her recklessness exposed her to a level of brutality and danger she had not experienced before – culminating in a savage attack on her by an aggrieved client for apparent betrayal. It was a valuable lesson for Amina: she must choose her options more carefully in future.

The next risky venture came through one of her favourite regulars, known simply as Don Pedro. For years he had retained Amina solely for sexual gratification and did not mix pleasure with business. He did not reveal much about himself, but kept Amina under close watch. All Amina knew about him was that Don Pedro was mega-rich and that he had consistently been her highest paymaster. Unbeknown to her, however, Don Pedro, Big Daddy and Elizabeth were business associates who ran a huge drug-running operation and other illicit activities. Elizabeth was a junior partner whose role included drug distribution and the grooming of young girls for the gang's sexual gratification, and for drug-trafficking if they could make the grade. Don Pedro was the drug kingpin in the city, a notorious manipulator and a deadly brute. He had monitored and watched Amina's every move, with spies dotted around the city, and he waited patiently for her to mature for his business. The 'nice guy' image, the money and the expensive gifts were an investment designed to keep Amina within the scope of his radar.

Don Pedro came to town after four months abroad and as usual called her to hookup with him in his hotel suite. Amina was ecstatic because Don Pedro was her highest-paying client, one of the few men who paid her in dollars, and the only man who could keep her for three consecutive days with the expectation of expensive gifts and a handbag stuffed with bundles of dollars. As she headed to his hotel, she was convinced that this would be the usual ritual of him enjoying a monopoly on her time, with the prospect of a huge reward at the end.

Unfortunately for her, this time Don Pedro wanted more than the pleasure of her body. He told her that he intended to offer her a job that would involve travelling and living abroad, and would create a huge opportunity for her to earn an income far larger than the peanuts she was getting for her 'personal services'. He claimed that the job would open a gateway to riches beyond her wildest dreams. He had watched her over the years, he said, and had come to the conclusion that in addition to being beautiful and intelligent, she was also smart, trustworthy, very confident and fearless. He was, however, worried that Amina might not have the ability to cope with the level of risk involved. Rewards, he said, were always commensurate with risk levels. Amina immediately fell into his arms, pleading for this rare chance to work for him, travel abroad and be mega-rich. She declared her willingness and capacity to manage any level of risk for him.

On hearing that reassurance, Don Pedro pulled out a package wrapped in plastic film and containing a white powder. He placed it on the table. 'What the hell is that?' Amina demanded to know. He told her it was cocaine, and proceeded to reveal to her that his great wealth came from the proceeds of crime, that he dealt drugs and was in fact the drug king in the city with unimpeded access to every security chief in the state, the director of the public prosecution service and the chief judge. He further claimed that these 'pillars of the state' played ball with him and showed solidarity in times of trouble to ensure that he remained untouchable. It was safe to work for him, he said, because the effects of his power, influence and high-society contacts would trickle favourably down to all his 'disciples' on the streets. He told Amina that everyone who worked for him was very rich, and if she worked for him too, she would become mega-rich.

Amina gave careful consideration to the risks associated with the offer, but concluded that these risks were minimal and, in any event, the benefits outweighed the dangers. She took confidence and comfort from Don Pedro's experience, contacts, power and influence to allay any lingering doubts.

To gauge her bravery and readiness to take high-level risks, Don Pedro encouraged Amina to take part in a drug orgy. If Amina was going to work in the drug business, he announced, she must be a user. This unexpected condition came as a shock to her, and for a moment she was paralysed. But she quickly gathered her thoughts and promised to experiment with drugs next time they met, in the hope that this would buy her time to take advice from Elizabeth. Her response, however, provoked anger from Don Pedro, who was accustomed to immediate compliance with his orders.

Suddenly there was a knock at the door and there, to Amina's surprise, was Elizabeth herself. Amina was further amazed when Elizabeth proceeded without any hesitation to prepare the drugs for them to use. Elizabeth was clearly not a newcomer to drug use or dealing.

Elizabeth proceeded to make two confessional statements that sent shockwaves through Amina. First, she confirmed her association with Big Daddy and Don Pedro as part of an international drug and prostitution cartel. Second, she now revealed that ever since her first meeting with Amina she had spent time, effort and resources on grooming the young girl for her own purposes. Now that Amina had reached this level, Elizabeth had accomplished her assigned mission and it was up to Amina to become as rich as her ambition and heart desired. She concluded by saying, ominously, 'There are no freebies or free lunches in life. Use what you have to get what you need. So don't let me down by wasting my years of commitment and loyalty to you, and always remember our oath.'

Faced with the combined persuasion from two of the most influential figures in her life apart from her mother, Amina inevitably crumbled under the sheer weight of the pressure. From that day, her life spiralled into a destructive whirl of drug-dealing, trafficking and abuse.

10

A Downward Spiral

Amina's decision that fateful night to agree to work for Don Pedro and to use illicit drugs defined the direction of both her personal life and her business empire. By making that decision she effectively accepted a life sentence, wedged between drug gangs and the law enforcement authorities. As far as Don Pedro and his gang were concerned, she had consented to being held hostage in a world dominated by drugs, abuse, violence and the constant threat of death. To the law enforcement agents, her decision meant a life in continuous danger of arrest, prosecution and imprisonment.

Don Pedro kick-started Amina's employment with yet another round of oath-taking rituals. This time she was taken to an allegedly powerful *juju* shrine with a frightening reputation of dispensing 'fair' justice and appropriate punishment in equal measures. Interestingly, the *juju* priest had trained and worked in the Western world as a medical doctor, but he held firm to his traditional beliefs, eventually abandoning his job and answering the call to become a *juju* priest. He was said to have been chosen for the role in the old, traditional way during a private ceremony involving *juju,* native doctors and the community elders. The chosen priest was then contacted through his family, and he returned home to perform his new functions. Refusal could not be contemplated: that would have meant calamity to his family beyond comprehension.

The oath Amina was made to take prohibited disclosure of trade secrets to third parties, betrayal, disloyalty, disobedience, cheating, deceit, lies and actions likely to damage the parties' interests. Breach of the oath would mean automatic attraction of the *juju's* anger, in the form of a slow and painful death, insanity or severe paralysis, with wider consequences for other family members. Once again, the primary aim of engaging Amina in this type of oath-taking was to instil perpetual fear in her mind, commanding control over her, and ensuring her loyalty, trust and confidence.

The entire plan for the drug operation and her specific role was then revealed to Amina in detail. The grand plan was to train Amina in every aspect of the cartel's national and international drug, prostitution and human trafficking operations. Later, at the appropriate time, she would be upgraded to 'associate member' of the cartel. Associate membership meant that she would be qualified and trusted to manage critical and sensitive nerve centres of the cartel's activities such as recruitment and training, as well as handling finances through an intricate worldwide web of secret accounts, money-holding centres and transfer methods designed to circumvent the various national and international money-laundering laws.

First, she needed training designed to teach her vital trade secrets and to toughen her up with a view to preparing her to remain fearless and ruthless, to withstand interrogation by the authorities and to be able to make tough decisions in difficult situations. The second phase required Amina to prove her toughness on the streets by achieving a set of targets which included the distribution of certain volumes of drugs through her girls. The third phase involved trafficking drugs from South America into European cities, working in conjunction with other agents. The final phase would see her based permanently in Europe as a *Madam* responsible for managing the receipt and distribution of human cargoes shipped to work as prostitutes and slave labour. She would also be expected to receive drugs from traffickers, to manage the distribution of those drugs and to repatriate all the proceeds to Nigeria via a network of well-established routes. Her bosses hoped that such a full cycle of experience would make Amina a complete all-rounder in the business.

Amina completed her discipline and toughness training within the allotted time and was then given targets to achieve on the streets, also within a stipulated time frame. While she worked on achieving those goals, it became obvious that her new dependency on drugs was having serious negative effects on her life and her business. Her behaviour spiralled dangerously out of control as her usual charisma and courteous mannerisms were replaced by arrogance, sauciness and an abusive attitude. She had been known and admired for her ability to plan, analyse and organize operations, but that was replaced by a 'don't care' attitude in every aspect of her activities. Unsurprisingly, her clients deserted her in droves and the income from her personal services dwindled at an alarming rate. Relationships with the girls she depended on for referral jobs, which formed a significant slice of her income, also suffered. She began to be greedy and took to charging excessive commission. In some cases she owed money to the girls, which in turn caused them to ask for advance payment. Others refused to go on her referral jobs when she called.

Despite her problems, Amina still accomplished her targets in record time, primarily because of her good network of girls and clients who were making huge returns from drug sales. To ensure effectiveness and compliance, she used the services of 'drug enforcers' who employed a combination of violence, intimidation, harassment and bullying to achieve results – particularly targeting those who refused to deal in or use drugs, those who were reluctant to go on referral jobs, or those she considered to be disloyal or disrespectful. Most of her girls ended up trapped in a vicious cycle of making money and then using it to feed their drug addiction.

Don Pedro was very impressed with Amina's perform-ance, so he proceeded to procure all the necessary travel documents to get her to Europe. Her family were told that she was going abroad for some compulsory on-the-job training that would boost her career prospects. Don Pedro and Elizabeth organized a farewell party at Elizabeth's home for close family friends and 'work' colleagues.

Soon after that, Amina made her journey to the Spanish city of Madrid, where she was provided with accommo-dation and introduced to the people who reported to the overall drug king in the area. She quickly settled down. A few weeks later, she was briefed and sent off on her first trip to South America. Her journeys were sometimes direct, but at other times she was routed through a third country. Her first trip went well and the pay was high. For several months she travelled successfully to and fro, carrying drugs. There were a few near misses which she managed to come through safely due to a combination of luck and sheer wit and charm. By then, Amina was beginning to be familiar to airport staff as a frequent traveller, so her bosses felt the time was right to reduce the level of her exposure and take her out of circulation for the time being. Amina was relieved by the decision: she felt she had done her time as a trafficker. She became a resident agent based in Barcelona, where she was soon introduced to the big guns on her patch.

Her time in Barcelona was hugely successful both for her bosses and for herself. Her personal finances back home remained very healthy and profitable, being exceptionally well managed by her mother, who provided her with regular updates. Amina also made a decent personal fortune while in Europe, which she quietly tucked away in her Nigerian bank account or hid in her Nigerian home in foreign currency. But her personal life was marred by excessive drug abuse.

She still managed to impress her bosses, however, successfully receiving large shipments of drugs from traffickers and organizing a series of shipments to other Spanish and European cities with astonishing ease. Perhaps her most successful activities involved human trafficking and the management of prostitution activities across Europe. She was the *Madam* for the cartel in Spain with a duty to receive young girls shipped into Spain to work as domestic servants or prostitutes. Amina also organized safe accommodation and secret private brothels where prostitutes worked under strict control, conducted by violence, bullying and intimidation. She also arranged the necessary paperwork for those prostitutes meant for trans-shipment to other European cities. She or her nominees were paid directly by clients and employers for the services provided by the prostitutes and domestic servants.

Her successes in Spain, together with her general experiences in prostitution, persuaded the cartel to post Amina to Italy as their official *Madam*. The profit margin was said to be good for each of the girls the cartel successfully smuggled to Italy. Each was sold on arrival for between 30,000-35,000 euros and for those who decided to work, they would each be given 18-24 months to repay between 50,000-60,000 euros as the cost of assisting them to Italy. Thereafter each girl would be free to work for herself.

For Amina, everything was going in the right direction until she learnt that 20 girls she was expecting on a particular shipment were among 110 others whose boat had capsized off the coast of Italy. The sad news left her utterly devastated because she had always advocated against this aspect of human trafficking due to this kind of tragedy and the degree of delays, hunger, starvation, imprisonment, violence, abuse and rape that these women suffer along the way. Her posting to Italy also exposed her to another disturbing experience about the hazards, appalling working conditions and other challenges the girls face on the job. Her experiences in Italy had a profound effect on her, triggering a holistic assessment of her role and involvement in perpetuating this human misery and tragedy. She accepted her role and complicity in this heinous crime against humanity.

The posting to Europe was largely successful and

trouble free for Amina for some time – until her luck ran out during a joint sting operation by the authorities. Amina was in Spain on the order of the cartel to attend a crucial meeting with her bosses from Nigeria, Spain, Holland and the UK. But, uknown to Amina and the cartel bosses, the US Drug Enforcement Agency (DEA), in conjunction with their Columbian and Spanish counterparts, was working on a notorious South American drug cartel when they intercepted a telephone conversation between the cartel and their Spanish dealers regarding drug shipments. During the operation, which lasted five months, the authorities intercepted communications and followed the trails of shipments between the cartel, several traffickers, couriers, dealers and drug barons in Spain. Amina's group suddenly came within the radar of the authorities and were subjected to intense scrutiny. This culminated in a simultaneous raid at various addresses in Madrid and Barcelona.

Amina was arrested at one of the houses with some others, but luckily for her only a small quantity of drugs and some cash was seized at her address later. A large amount of drugs was found at other addresses, with a street value of ten million euros. All those arrested were prosecuted, found guilty and sentenced to various terms of imprisonment, with the big players receiving longer sentences. Amina was also found guilty and was given a lighter prison sentence of five years with a deportation order on her release.

Jail was an alien world for Amina, accustomed to a high life of luxury, authority, fashion, parties, drug abuse and freedom. The prospect of a five-year jail sentence triggered a serious physical, psychological and emotional breakdown as she began to question her desire to live on. She worried about her family, about her money, about her business and the loss of territory this jail term would bring. It seemed to her that the clock had stopped. As the prison gates slammed shut behind her and the days and nights suddenly became longer, Amina inevitably sought refuge in the drugs that had led her into jail in the first place.

There was no communication or help from Elizabeth, Don Pedro or Big Daddy, except for a short, anonymous note delivered soon after her arrest that read, 'Don't say a word, or else.' Amina felt lonely and abandoned. It seemed that despite the connections Don Pedro had boasted about, his influence did not extend across the Sahara Desert and the sea to Spain.

As the days turned to weeks she came to the realization that her new situation was real and not a mere nightmare. She accepted her fate and tried to adjust to life in jail, knowing that she might be released early for good behaviour. At least, she comforted herself, her money was being well managed by her mother at home. She kept her misfortune entirely secret from the family, fabricating different stories to mask her difficulties and dreaming up a variety of excuses for her inability to make her usual frequent calls.

Amina spent the rest of her time in prison binging on drugs with shared needles. After refusing drug addiction treatment for the first three years, she started a drug rehab programme twelve months before she was due to be released – but by this time she had been infected with the AIDS virus. When she finally reached the end of her jail term, she was released and deported back to Nigeria in accordance with the terms of her sentence.

11

Amina's Return Home

The news of Amina's imminent arrival back in Nigeria was greeted with jubilation by her family. They knew nothing of the truth, and were simply joyful that her claim to have successfully completed her 'on-the-job training' abroad would now further enhance her career aspirations, and would most certainly guarantee an even better future for the family. She had been a long time away, leaving both a physical and an emotional vacuum in the family she had left behind. Naturally Ada and her excited family were at a fever pitch of expectation as they waited in the arrivals hall of the airport to welcome Amina home. Their noisy anticipation reached a crescendo when Amina finally appeared. It was an emotional reunion as they all screamed, hugged, kissed and cried tears of joy.

With the help of intensive treatment in the prison rehab centre over the previous twelve months, Amina looked deceptively beautiful and healthy, showing no signs of the illness and drug dependency that had plagued her young life in recent times.

Amina returned to a city that had gone through huge transformation as a result of rapid development during the years she had been away. The personal business she had entrusted to her mother's control remained healthy and her bank account was buoyant. Ada had finished her law degree, had gone to law school and been called to the bar, and was now running a thriving law firm. Amina's siblings had all graduated from university and completed their national youth service training. They were now assisting in running parts of her (above-board) business.

However, her attempt to make contact and square things up with Elizabeth, Big Daddy and Don Pedro failed. Apparently Amina had passed her sell-by date and was no longer useful as far as they were concerned. Presumably they now saw her as a liability and a huge security risk. Her bosses did not want to draw unnecessary attention to themselves or their operations. Amina was bitter about the way she had been abandoned and left without support from the time of her arrest, throughout her prison sentence and since her arrival back in Nigeria. Why had she been left without back-up? She wanted answers, but received none.

She started to question the oath-taking rituals. What had they been about, ultimately? All that talk about loyalty, betrayal and trust, and the threat of dire consequences for any breach of the oath, had driven her commitment to take risks and slave for her bosses all those years. But she had received no loyalty in return. It was another example, she concluded, of how the masculine world operated – and she and her family were left to pay the price. Her bitterness and frustration drove her to the point of being ready to expose and sink the cartel for good. She was prevented from taking that open course of action, however, by the knowledge of their destructive power and ruthlessness. Understandably, she feared for the safety of her mother and siblings.

Had she only had herself to consider, Amina was certain that she would be willing to make the ultimate sacrifice of her life in order to bring the cartel down. She acknowledged privately that she had contributed to her current difficult situation herself by voluntarily committing herself to doing whatever it took to lift her family from poverty. She remained joyful and without any regrets that this part of her mission had been accomplished. Her only regret was that only now did she realize that one of her own kind, Elizabeth, had conspired all along with the masculine world to bring this latest misery to her family. Elizabeth herself, she recognized, had been motivated throughout by selfishness, greed and personal interests. What could Amina, alone in the world, now do to wreak some revenge on those who had conspired against her? Armed with all the experience she had gained, and having learned a hard lesson about selfishness and self-interest, Amina resolved to conduct her mission with all the ruthlessness and fearlessness she had learned to wield during her training by the cartel.

Filled with anger, hatred and bitterness at the way she had been rejected, betrayed and abandoned by those she had trusted, loved and slaved for, Amina planned to unleash a painful punishment on the society that had made that possible – but in a way which she hoped would not give any cause to her merciless former employers to punish her own family. She was going to resume her runs operation, but this time with vengeance and destruction in mind. She would seek retribution on the society and the masculine world that had caused her family to suffer pain, death, humiliation and degradation simply on the basis of their gender. To achieve this, she set out to infect as many clients as possible with the AIDS virus before the end of her own life.

With plenty of street experience behind her, backed up by her looks and her wealth, Amina trawled her old familiar grounds, now colonized by a new breed of clients who had no clue who she was but were simply mesmerized by her beauty. She adopted a new identity and steadily began to attract new clients from all walks of life – young university graduates, handsome working-class single men, young married men and married middle-aged men. She offered all kinds of sexual acts, free of charge and without any protection. She hoped that her target groups would help her to spread the deadly AIDS virus to vulnerable groups such as wives, long-term partners and single women who sold their bodies to other men. For those clients who were conscious of the dangers of AIDS, HIV and other sexually transmitted diseases and who insisted on protective sex, she would tempt them with a convincing storyline to attract sympathy – telling them a sob story about her partner's impotence or inability to make her pregnant. If that failed, she would offer them astronomical sums of money just to get her way. Sadly for the majority of these men, she met with phenomenal success as the news of her 'generosity' spread around the city like a bush fire. Men flocked in for a piece of her body and her money.

In the midst of all this, Amina relapsed. Hiding herself away from her family for months, she sucked herself deeper into drug abuse, overdosing on several occasions and going for weeks without taking her AIDS medication. From time to time she called her family and claimed to be busy on projects in another city, and her family blindly accepted her excuses for not returning home. One fateful day, a hotel cleaner found her on the floor of her room and raised the alarm. Amina was rushed to a clinic, where she remained in a coma for two days. On the third day she came round and demanded urgently to see her mother. With little strength left in her, she managed to reveal her identity and her mother's name and address.

Ada arrived at the clinic, but barely recognized her emaciated daughter. Shocked and fighting back tears, Ada demanded to know what had happened to her. With a little smile, Amina now made a frank and complete confession to her mother about the secret life she had been lured into by Elizabeth – the prostitution, the drug abuse, the drug-trafficking mission from South America to Europe, the jail sentence and eventual deportation back to Nigeria.

This horrifying news plunged Ada into paralysed numbness, but Amina spoke on. 'Mum, I'm dying of AIDS and drug abuse. I have a limited time to live. The family should celebrate my life and appreciate my personal commitment to them instead of wasting time crying. Our misfortune has been to live in a society that has treated us as second-class citizens by engineering the environment, culture, tradition, religion and law to our detriment on the basis of our gender. Poverty has been the other source of our suffering. I was powerless to change the fact of our gender, but I knew I could do something to eliminate our poverty. I made a conscious decision after Halima's death to be the sacrificial lamb for the good of the family. I declared war on poverty and opted to do whatever it would take to free the family from its grip.

'I have no regrets whatsoever for anything I've done, because I've made the family wealthy and secured your future: you now have the freedom to make choices in life without influence from men or society. For the future, your granddaughters can now be empowered through education and I hope that they'll be part of their own generation's fight for women's liberation. I've accomplished my goal and enjoyed the best the world can offer. I can die as a happy woman. Please, Mum, don't hold grudges, and don't blame Elizabeth. She has a sad story too. She was also the victim of fate and cultural conspiracy.'

Rather than wasting precious time feeling sorry for her, Amina urged her mother to use the wealth she had accumulated to build a lasting legacy so that the causes of her pains and her journey through life might be remembered. She asked Ada to direct all her energy towards addressing issues that undermined women's development, rights and freedom in society. She wanted her mother to focus on empowering young girls by helping them acquire academic education; fighting against early and forced marriages; fighting against domestic violence; fighting against child labour, particularly against girls of school age being employed as 'housegirls'; helping women who were victims of drug and alcohol abuse; and sponsoring female legislators during elections.

Later that same day, Amina's health deteriorated. Concluding that she had no hope of pulling through, the doctors advised Ada to prepare for the worst. Amina passed away that evening in her mother's arms, aged twenty-eight.

For Ada, Amina's death was devastating. She was distraught that her daughter had deemed it fit and proper to demonstrate such a level of personal sacrifice for the good of the family. The loss was unbearable. It was, of course, made worse by the fact that Amina had died of

AIDS, which still had a lot of stigma attached to it, largely due to ignorance. Ada knew that she and her family would once again become the subject of vicious gossip in their community. As she had once done on her own behalf, Ada now laid the blame for her daughter's suffering on fate, poverty, society and tradition.

Contrary to Amina's advice in her dying moments, Ada was also very critical of Elizabeth for deceiving her family and manipulating Amina to her death. She recalled her early suspicions of Elizabeth during their initial encounters. At the time she had questioned Elizabeth's motives and felt uneasy at her extreme generosity. She had sensed that Elizabeth's account of the source of her immense wealth did not add up, and had felt that something was definitely odd about a beautiful and excessively wealthy woman who did not have a man or a family member by her side. Now she blamed herself for not probing further. If only she had acted on her suspicions before it was too late!

Ada reflected on other occasions when things had begun to show signs of improvement in her life, and then something tragic would happen to shatter her world once more. It had started with the trouble over her education. Then her marriage had broken down in the worst possible way. Her business in the city had also collapsed. Now her beautiful daughter Amina was dead.

Amina was buried at her father's home in a simple ceremony in accordance with the instructions she had left behind. A huge number of people attended the burial to pay their last respects, including representatives from all the charity organizations funded by her wealth. Elizabeth, Big Daddy and Don Pedro failed to attend.

12

Ada the Liberator

Ada returned to her base in the city still suffering the effects of the loss of her daughter. She disengaged herself from all activities for many weeks, spiralling downward into depression. She felt she carried the whole blame for not acting promptly and doing all that was necessary to prevent her daughter's destruction. How could she have allowed herself to be fooled for years by the elaborate lies which Elizabeth and Amina herself had concocted to cover up her daughter's secret life? How had she failed to spot the tell-tale signs of the truth? If only she had been more careful! She had failed to ask the obvious questions, she had failed to dig deeper – when surely she should have been suspicious of the rapid development in the family fortunes, taken together with her previous doubts about Elizabeth's wealth. More hurtful even than that was the thought of her innocent teenage daughter making money from prostitution, then from drug-dealing, and serving a five-year sentence in a foreign prison – while Ada herself was blithely conducting her daily business, sleeping in luxury every night, entirely ignorant of the plight of her daughter.

Nonetheless, with the support of her two remaining

daughters, doctors and close family friends, Ada gradually pulled through her worst period. Over time she regained her energy, and turned back to Amina's final wishes. She remembered her own previous attempt to start a liberation fight, which had been defeated before it began by her father's decision to force her in to an arranged marriage. She suddenly realized that now there were no more serious impediments to her youthful dreams. She now had the money, power, knowledge and time to mobilize political and social support. Years had passed since she had first conceived her liberation movement, and things had moved on in the right direction, but there was so much still to be done in terms of driving positive changes to the way society perceived women's rights, freedom and roles. She wanted once again to create national awareness of women's issues. She urgently wanted to generate interest amongst women of all ages and from all walks of life, encouraging them to participate in the fight. Focusing on this project, she hoped, would help her turn away from her personal pain and use Amina's death to put joy on the faces of a generation of young girls and women.

Over the following weeks and months Ada summoned a formidable pool of experts and charged them to put their considerable experience to good use in support of her agenda on women's issues. Brainstorming sessions brought the team to agree that they must fight on several fronts: women were generally suffering abuse, humiliation, marginalization, victimization, oppression, prejudice, stigmatization and the denial of rights, privileges and freedom. They identified common barriers in Nigerian society which impeded women's development, and which germinated from religious beliefs and practices, artificial cultural tradition, discriminatory laws, natural or biological conditions, poverty, and generational attitudes.

Religion and culture together had arbitrarily created roles, responsibilities and expectations for men and women and had accordingly allotted different values to them, leading to an impression that the role of men was of greater importance than that of women. As a consequence, male children had gained an unfair advantage over female children in the family setting. This situation was often abused, particularly when family resources were limited. The needs of male children were then given disproportionate preference, resulting in a feeling of inferiority amongst women in the family, which was undoubtedly replicated in the wider society.

Society's perception of the role and contribution of women dictated the choices women were able to make (or the choices made for them), limited the opportunities available to them, and generally determined how they led their lives. This clearly caused obstructions in the general development of women.

Ada and her team also agreed that childlessness in marriage was another classic example of how cultural barriers caused women to suffer victimization and marginalization, both in the family and in wider society. Childless women, for example, were often denied some or all inheritance rights when they became widows, irrespective of their contribution to their late husband's wealth.

The team also found that women who had only female children often suffered domestic abuse at the hands of their partners, who blamed them for failing to produce male children. Ada gave her team an account of how she and her daughters had suffered extreme abuse, emotional torture and humiliation by family members, neighbours and the community at large. In addition, female children were not accorded automatic right of inheritance on their father's death, particularly if they were already married. Family members readily and conveniently activated this weapon in their determination to grab the available wealth. Female children might also be denied the right to proper education if they were still very young on the death of their father, because society expected them to marry out of the family at a certain age. So, for example, if their uncle was poor and had male children of his own, he would rather use the inherited money and other property to fund his male children's education instead of investing in girls who would marry and leave the family home.

The team also identified the sad position of some unmarried women who suffered stigmatization and the denial of certain basic rights in some parts of society. If they had children out of wedlock, those children also suffered injustice, being regarded as having no identity and no rights of their own.

Ada explicitly identified poverty as playing a critical role in affecting women's development. She explained to the team how, in her own experience, it had drastically limited her opportunities, influenced the choices she had to make, and removed her independence, leading to many layers of suffering. Ada and her team concluded that lack of basic means could make women heavily reliant on a male-dominated society for existence and survival, which in turn rendered them vulnerable.

Female circumcision, they found, was a further example of how the culture and the masculine world tended to create artificial barriers designed to control and dictate women's behaviour. Without any shred of medical or scientific evidence, some parts of society stuck to the claim that uncircumcised women were more easily sexually aroused and therefore more likely to commit adultery. So, to stop women enjoying sex and to control the 'sluttish sexual activities' that might lead to disorder in the community, some cultures decreed that every female child should be circumcised.

The team identified the fact that general human behaviour and attitudes were just as significant as poverty in terms of impeding women's development. The artificial barriers placed by society in terms of laws, religious decrees and cultural beliefs over generations, helped shape behaviour and attitudes prejudicial to women.

At the end of the review process, Ada and her team had identified some crucial cultural, religious and behavioural barriers to women's development. Moving on, the team then tried to identify their own strengths, weaknesses and opportunities, and any likely threats to the successful implementation of their project. They also looked at the political, social and other environmental issues that might adversely affect their plans. At that point they found themselves in a position to set out their mission and their goals, both long and short term. They established their target audience, highlighted the enormity of the task ahead, and laid out a step-by-step approach that would prepare them for all foreseeable challenges along the way.

The team planned to create maximum awareness on women's issues through education aimed at changing the old perceptions and habits that had blighted the lives of women for so many generations. It aimed to work in partnership with government and other relevant agencies, civil society groups, established women's groups and NGOs, professional bodies and even, if possible, traditional regional rulers. They also recognized the need to enlist the support of women in powerful positions, as well as female celebrities. Finally, they hoped to use the legal system if necessary to seek justice and to ensure compliance.

Although women generally faced huge difficulties in Nigerian society, Ada and her team realized that some women were definitely more vulnerable than others. As a starting point, therefore, they agreed to concentrate much of their resources on the most vulnerable – divorcees, widows, those fleeing or suffering domestic violence and other abuses, rape victims, drug addicts, alcoholics, abused young girls, children employed as housemaids or house girls, girls used by their parents or other family members to sell products on the streets, and young girls involved in the sex trade.

After months of meticulous planning, Ada felt that it was appropriate to jump start the entire project with the establishment of an education foundation. She regarded this as her 'pet project', and it was very close to her heart for several reasons. In addition to fulfilling Amina's wishes, Ada was determined to ensure that young girls would not miss out on the opportunity to acquire education, or be forced into early marriages at school age due to lack of money. If such a foundation had existed earlier, Ada herself might not have been driven into an arranged marriage, and later her daughter Halima might also have been able to stay at school out of harm's way.

The purpose of her foundation, therefore, was to empower young girls from poor backgrounds through education. She hoped this would help them access better opportunities for the future: they would be able to make better choices, be independent, enjoy more freedom, and ultimately take the long struggle for liberation to the next level. In addition to providing primary and secondary education, Ada's foundation also offered scholarships to young girls who attended other schools, as well as universities. The foundation also sponsored other young women from the orphanage and refuge centre who were not in formal education, but who wished to acquire vocational skills to help them engage in private enterprise.

An orphanage was set up according to Amina's last wishes. It provided a warm and loving home for highly vulnerable categories of young girls, including those who were motherless, abandoned or homeless, those fleeing abuse and roaming the streets, rescued domestic servants or child labourers, and girls found selling goods on the street or forced into the sex trade. The orphanage and the education foundation worked together to support these girls and gradually ease them back into schools.

Another key project was a women's refuge centre, named after Amina. Again, it was the kind of resource that Ada wished had been available for her, either when she had been resisting the pressure from her parents to abandon her education and marry, or when she had fled her married home to escape from domestic abuse. The centre was specifically set up to rescue women fleeing abuse from their parents or husbands, those seeking to avoid forced marriages, women who had been chased out of their married homes, domestic maids fleeing from abusive employers, and young girls thrown out of their family homes because of unplanned pregnancy.

The refuge centre also played a significant role in the prosecution of cases involving those who had offended against the women in the centre. Working in conjunction with Ada's law firm and the state prosecutors, the centre helped to gather vital evidence against the offenders and assisted the victims to provide witness statements. It also provided general witness and victim support, including protection, counselling, an advisory service and assistance with court attendance. Perhaps more important was the training that the centre helped to provide – in basic reading and writing skills and wider education; vocational training to help women set up their own businesses or gain other employment; and in advice on domestic violence and women's rights, equipping them to deal with challenges they might meet outside the refuge by training them to recognize different faces and deal with domestic violence, ensuring that they knew where they could seek protection, advice and support.

Lastly, the centre organized a training programme for an army of volunteer local champions, agents for change and feminist groups – the 'foot soldiers' working at grass-roots level. These groups went out to target identified audiences in their various localities, creating a higher awareness of domestic violence and its detrimental effects on the victims, their communities and the wider society, and promoting positive changes in behaviour, attitudes and beliefs.

In her dying moments, Amina also left specific instructions with her mother to use part of her wealth to help other young girls suffering from drug addiction and AIDS/HIV. Ada and her team accordingly established a facility in Amina's memory called the AIDS and Drug

Rehabilitation Centre, fully kitted out with up-to-date equipment and well trained staff.

Ada was sadly aware that Nigeria was ranked as one of the most corrupt nations in the world, with some public officers stealing public money on a monumental scale. With little or no effort made by the leaders to create jobs, the level of unemployment was disproportionately high amongst the female population, particularly young girls. Trapped in a cycle of poverty and lack of education, many were easily lured by the money available in the sex trade. Although the majority of women apparently went into prostitution voluntarily, some were forced into it by demanding parents who expected them to use whatever means they could to help provide for the family. Others were simply persuaded by friends to make easy money, while some were lured by criminal gangs who exploited their vulnerability. Because of their naivety and lack of sex education, majority of these young girls engaged in sexual activities without protection. Some were raped; some had unprotected sex unaware that their partners had AIDS or were HIV positive. As a result, sexually transmitted diseases and AIDS/HIV may have reached epidemic proportions in a country that lacked adequate medical care. There were few specialist AIDS/HIV professionals or facilities in the country, and a totally inadequate awareness campaign. The stigma attached to the condition also prevented sufferers from admitting they had AIDS in the first place, leaving them reluctant to attend public places like hospitals or clinics to receive treatment.

Ada's team took care to involve government health agencies and her NGO in the setting up of their AIDS and drug rehabilitation centre: their aim was for it to operate within the main public health arena. It was agreed that the relevant NGO would provide strategic leadership and support to the centre. As a result, the centre was allowed to use its high-quality facilities to run government-supported programmes on AIDS and HIV, dispensing free drug, counselling and advisory services and treatment in a private environment. It was also used by the national health ministry as a centre for training specialist AIDS/HIV staff, sometimes with the input of international experts. A volunteer recruitment and training programme on AIDS/HIV awareness was set up so that local agents for change could go back to their own communities after training and spread the message about safe practice.

Ada's lifelong ambition to be a lawyer had finally been realized when Amina's wealth made the completion of her studies possible at last. Influenced by her own experiences, she had set up her own law firm, specializing in criminal law, family law and mediation/arbitration. She now used her law firm as the anchor for her entire humanitarian project, employing its expertise in offering help and advice to the various support centres her team set up. She also coordinated all the assistance they provided to the state prosecution service. She played a central role in the training on women's rights and domestic violence, and helped countless women to seek and obtain justice. She secured fair settlements for the women and custody of the children in a number of high-profile divorce cases, and successfully defended and claimed proper inheritance rights for widows. She also assisted the state in bringing to justice perpetrators of domestic abuse.

The NGO wing of Ada's vast project was formidable in its work and purpose. It was the engine room and think-tank for the whole humanitarian operation. With a talented team in place, it provided strategic leadership and engineered winning strategies for the multiple organizations under its control. As the 'public face'of the group, it provided start-up funds and organized all the regulatory registration and operational licences for each of the support centres. It also conducted fundraising activities, gaining contributions from the public; local, state and federal governments; corporate bodies and international organizations to supplement what it dispensed itself to each of the centres. At the core of its operations was the national campaign to heighten awareness of women's issues, including roles, rights, freedoms, equality, domestic abuse, rape and education.

To achieve all this, Ada and her team worked hard to enlist the support of those who wielded influence in politics, civil society and the world of sport and entertainment. They identified ingenious strategies to mobilize massive support from women and others in powerful positions at local, state and federal levels, to help move things in their favour. Their aim was to persuade legislators to abolish out-of-date or discriminatory laws against women, and introduce new laws to prohibit traditional practices that impinged on the rights and freedom of women. Equally, they worked to strengthen and enforce existing legislation that was already favourable to women. Another vital role they played was in the effort to attitudes and practices within specific public departments such as the police, judiciary and health services – for example in the way they dealt with reported cases of rape, domestic violence and forced marriage, or in the support offered in cases of breast cancer, infant mortality and HIV/AIDS.

Perhaps the biggest role of the organization was in the mobilization and training of a dedicated army of field volunteers at the local level. In association with Ada's law firm and other centres, the NGO periodically earmarked huge resources for volunteer training programmes on all aspects of women's rights and freedom. The volunteers also received specific training on domestic violence, how to recognize its different forms, how to deal with it and where to seek help. The volunteers were then sent back to their own towns and villages, where they would train other volunteers to drive home messages aimed at changing entrenched generational behaviour that was oppressive and highly prejudicial to women.

13

Rewarding Experience

For Ada, devoting so much of her time and energy to this huge project and witnessing the joy on the faces of the staff and those they helped at the end of each day brought much relief and an endless sense of accomplishment. That achievement was even more remarkable in such a conservative society considering her determination to win her arguments through a combination of gentle persuasion and superior reasoning. It was a moderate but extra-ordinarily effective brand of feminism – a sensible move away from the aggressive, extremist and 'male-bashing' feminism that tended only to alienate its targets. But she never forgot that these accomplishments would not have been possible without her daughter Amina's priceless sacrifice of her life, her future and her happiness in her selfless desire to right the wrong done to her family over the years.

At last, Ada's long-held ambition to become a successful lawyer and working mother, and to engage herself positively in the struggle for women's liberation in Nigeria had come to fruition. At the very least, her successes served to mitigate the tragedies she had suffered in her life. She was satisfied to know that her sacrifices, her pain and her dogged determination to see that her earlier experiences should not befall another family had generated the motivation, tenacity and burning desire to succeed on this huge project. Philosophically, she accepted that every event in life happens for a reason, and every disappointment ought to be treated as a potential blessing in disguise. She came to see her own bad experiences as valuable lessons in the realities of life, which she was able to convert positively for the benefit of so many other women. Because of that, Ada considered herself a winner and became a new convert to the old saying, 'Everyone is a winner, but some of us are disguised as losers, so don't let their appearance fool you.'

Over the years her successful humanitarian work attracted much attention and admiration from around the globe – she was celebrated as the modern face of feminism. Some called her a modern-day Mother Teresa, others saw her as a 'lioness', a 'liberator', and a supreme advocate for women's rights. In recognition of her immense contributions in the field of women's development, Nigeria bestowed on her a prestigious national honour and appointed her as the minister for women's affairs, which granted her even greater opportunities to pursue her work at a national level. That achievement was capped some months later by another continental award from the African Union. But the greatest recognition came on the glorious day when Ada, dressed elegantly in native African attire, addressed a full United Nations Assembly in New York. At the end of the long, standing ovation, Ada felt overwhelmed. With tears of joy streaming down her cheeks, she publicly dedicated her awards and her achievements to her late daughter, Amina.